THE UPTOWN KIDS

THE UPTOWN KIDS

STRUGGLE AND HOPE IN THE PROJECTS

TERRY WILLIAMS
AND
WILLIAM KORNBLUM

A GROSSET/PUTNAM BOOK
PUBLISHED BY G. P. PUTNAM'S SONS
NEW YORK

A Grosset/Putnam Book
Published by G. P. Putnam's Sons
Publishers Since 1838
200 Madison Avenue
New York, NY 10016

Library of Congress Cataloging-in-Publication Data

Williams, Terry M. (Terry Moses), date.
    The uptown kids : struggle and hope in the projects /
Terry Williams and William Kornblum.
        p.   cm.
    "A Grosset/Putnam book."
    Includes index.
    ISBN 0-399-13887-0 (alk. paper)
    1. Socially handicapped youth—New York (N.Y.) 2. Minority youth—New York
(N.Y.) 3. Narcotics and youth—New York (N.Y.) 4. Public housing—New York (N.Y.)
5. New York (N.Y.)—Social conditions.   I. Kornblum, William.   II. Title.
HV1437.N5W55   1994   93-47192 CIP
362.7′979607307471—dc20

The authors gratefully acknowledge permission to quote the lyrics on pages 106–8,
which are reprinted by permission of the publishers, Harvard University Press, from
*"Get Your Ass in the Water and Swim Like Me": Narrative Poetry from Black Oral
Tradition* by Bruce Jackson, copyright © 1974 by the President and Fellows of
Harvard College; and the excerpt on pages 23–24, which is reprinted by permission
of the publishers, Random House, from *The Vertical Ghetto: Everyday Life in an Urban
Project* by William Moore, Jr., copyright © 1969.

Book design by H. Roberts
Map on page 29 by Howard R. Roberts

Printed in the United States of America
1   2   3   4   5   6   7   8   9   10

This book is printed on acid-free paper.

Acknowledgments

This book would not be possible without the efforts of young people from the projects. Our sincerest appreciation and heartfelt gratitude to Jamal Bailey, Gene Fields, Kahlil Hicks, Errol Kenya James, Akemi Kochiyama-Ladson, Epe Kgositsele, Sean Mackey, Joan Morgan, Yasin Muhammed, Nimboko, Tanya Parker, Budd Powell, Charisse Saunders, and Alexandro Smith.

We thank Val Coleman, Ron Metcalf, and Len Hopper at the New York City Housing Authority, and all managers, tenant association presidents, and tenant leaders who gave us the opportunity to interview tenant groups and project residents. Special thanks to Doreen Mack and Ruby Kitchen at Martin Luther King, Jr., Towers; Delores Stewart, Sandra Robeson, and Ethel Velez at J. W. Johnson Houses; Ron Cox, Marie Castellano, and Anna

Ayala at Carver; and James Grossman and Charmayne Innis at Drew Hamilton for the time they took out of their busy schedules. The Tenants Advisory Council was very helpful, especially Barbara Barber and Violet B. Hamilton. We particularly appreciate the time and effort of Professor Katherine Newman at Columbia University and two extremely capable student research assistants, Alicia Schmidt-Camacho and Marjorie Innocent.

Many people gave their time, energy, wisdom, and money to make this book a reality. The research began with a MacArthur Foundation grant in 1988, with the help of Richard Jessor, Tom Cook, William Wilson, Betty Hamburg, and others. In addition we received support from Eric Wanner, president of the Russell Sage Foundation.

We are indebted to others who contributed to the book in one way or another: Sharon Ellis and Edith Slade, for their photographs; Robert Simels, Peggy Raptis, and Dave Tougher, for their legal advice and support for the kids during crises; Maria Beltre, for her support and encouragement; Christina Head, for her organizing skills; John Goering, for his knowledge of housing; Herbert Gans, for his reading and excellent comments on the early manuscript; and Robert Merton, resident scholar at the Russell Sage Foundation, for his masterly editing and suggestions. Phillip Kasinitz also made invaluable suggestions.

We thank Ann Mische for her interviews and time spent with the kids; Gina Kolata for her mentoring; and Louise Gauthier for her helpful observations about graffiti. Deborah Prothrow-Stith was very thoughtful and offered encouragement and emotional support for the kids when they needed it most. Others who helped us include Rosa Carillo, Dave Isay, Rosa Landinez, Debbie Meier, Marie-Claude Nouy, Eric Pooley, Elaine Rivera, Jan Rosenberg, Toye Washington, the Black Student Leadership Network, and the Children's Defense Fund. We cannot thank Rona Cohen, Jane Isay's assistant, enough for her indefatigable work in getting the book to press.

This book would not have been possible without the support, patience, and understanding of our families. Bill's wife, Susan, and children, Noah, Eve, and Johanna, offered suggestions and encouragement, and helped when the uptown kids came calling. Terry's sisters, Sandra Smith and Janice Williams, and brother-in-law, Donald Smith, and his sons, Kahlil and Neruda, gave invaluable help and support.

Although many people helped this book get to its final stage, we take responsibility for its shortcomings.

To Jane Isay with love, respect and admiration

C O N T E N T S

INTRODUCTION

The Public Housing Opportunity

This book is the product of a twenty-year collaboration and friendship. We began working together in 1973 at the Graduate School of the City University of New York. One of us, Terry Williams, was a doctoral student and the other, William Kornblum, an assistant professor, of recent vintage. We collaborated on a series of research projects dedicated to the creation of federal seashores and national parks in the nation's metropolitan regions. In the ensuing years we have worked on more projects together than we can easily call to mind. But this one about young people growing up in Harlem public housing neighborhoods is close to our own experience with New York City. Its origins begin with our own personal biographies and with the social forces that brought us together in the first place.

13

Terry Williams's path to Harlem and to concern for its people began in the Deep South. Born in McComb, Mississippi, Terry is one of twelve children. His father was a plumber and well-known tradesman in the rural town and surrounding hamlets. His mother worked as a domestic and eventually became a celebrated dorm mother in the local college. All the Williams children worked hard to achieve financial and economic success. Some received advanced university degrees, while others have had successful careers in nonacademic fields and as homemakers. Williams family reunions typically gather more than a hundred members of the close-knit extended family. As teenagers Williams and his siblings became active in the civil rights movement locally, and even nationally. Through participation in the Southern Nonviolent Coordinating Committee, the Mississippi voter registration drives, endless meetings, demonstrations in cities and towns, Williams met people who encouraged him to come to New York for college. While attending the City University of New York, College of Staten Island, he worked on many civil rights campaigns and jobs. At one point he and his brother Michael were part of an effort by New York City civil rights groups who were attempting to integrate the infamously segregated construction trades. Williams was sent to be an apprentice ironworker. He had never expressed an interest in "high steel," but the wages were far more than he could have earned at the time doing anything else. And as the civil rights leaders knew, "he could pass any test sent his way." Now that he had a young family, including Audee, his wife, and Kahlil Zulu, his first son, the ironworker's wages were enticing. He was successful at the job, but that was something of a problem, for his interests were more in the direction of theater and poetry and social concerns. Working with Crossroads Africa in West Africa he had become fascinated with the changing society there. The prospect of the ironworker's trade as a career was far too confining. Mentors in Harlem and former professors at City University persuaded him to study sociology in graduate school, and thereby combine his talents in writing and social activism.

For much of the time Williams was in graduate school, he and his family lived in the Manhattanville Houses in Harlem, well known as one of the most politically active housing projects in the city. And for much of the time the tenants conducted rent strikes to obtain better services from the New York City Housing Authority. After a few years in the projects and some years in another neighborhood, Washington Heights, Williams moved back to Harlem, to a beautiful old apartment where he now resides and where many of the scenes described in this book occur. For many years Williams has tracked the lives of people he knows who have become enmeshed in the city's web of drug sales and consumption. His research has produced two influential and widely cited books, *The Cocaine Kids* (1989) and *Crack House* (1992). Now a professor of community studies and ethnography at the New School for Social Research in New York, he also develops programs to enrich the lives of young people in Harlem and other urban communities.

William Kornblum's path to writing about Harlem is more typical of the dedicated outsider. A native New Yorker whose parents were intellectuals and social activists, Kornblum learned early on about the confounding of race and class issues in American urban life. An intense two-year stint in the Peace Corps in the early 1960s, as a physics and chemistry teacher in a *lycée* in Abidjan, Ivory Coast, helped him to be comfortable as a minority white in a black world. The experience of life in the newly independent nations of Africa guided him toward the social sciences and graduate study at the University of Chicago, where he earned his doctorate in sociology. In Chicago during the later 1960s, Kornblum and his wife, Susan, a psychologist, joined the social movements and marched in historic political demonstrations. They lived and worked in the steel-mill community of South Chicago, where Kornblum conducted research for his dissertation and first book, *Blue Collar Community* (1974). South Chicago, at the mouth of the Calumet River, was then one of the nation's most celebrated areas of heavy industry and industrial unions. It was also a community that had experienced more than its share of bloody confrontations over integration in factories, neighborhoods, and schools. Kornblum's book became well known as a community study in the rich literature of American ethnic and race relations, much of which had been produced in the Chicago tradition of urban studies.

Poor minority families were hit especially hard by the dramatic loss of heavy industry in South Chicago and urban communities throughout the United States during the 1970s and 1980s. Their prospects for benefits-paying employment and for residential mobility worsened with the loss of millions of blue-collar jobs and the extension of the rust belt.

We are still living through the effects of this historic transformation in the economy of older industrialized nations. It is evident that people in New York and other major manufacturing cities who clawed and scraped their way in the 1960s and 1970s to relatively secure shelter in public housing are now bearing the worst burden of the post-industrial revolution. The shift to employment based on information and services rather than on the work of the body and hands narrows the range of options for less educated entrants into the labor force. The demand for ever higher levels of education places severe burdens on people who suffer from inadequate education. As community sociologists, we too are mightily influenced by these historic changes. Over the years our work has necessarily come to focus more on the conditions of young people with limited material resources who are caught in the crosscurrents of a rapidly changing urban world.

Our collaboration began in the early 1970s, with research on public use of former military bases as beaches, parks, and environmental areas. That broadened into an investigation of central urban communities such as Times Square where there is intense public use. With Vernon Boggs and colleagues at CUNY we conducted the first comprehensive study of lower Times Square and West 42nd Street for Roger Kennedy at The Ford Foundation. In 1979, soon after the research gained public attention, we were asked by Robert Schrank and Mitchell Svirdoff at Ford to conduct an ambitious comparative study of teenagers from representative low-income communities throughout the United States. Ultimately this became a youth employment program which we organized and ran, with funding from the Department of Labor. During this project we developed an appreciation for the young people's insights and their creativity in writing and speaking, and built their perceptions into *Growing Up Poor* (1985), a comparative study of the lives of teenagers and young adults in several American communities. We employed, and surveyed, young people in New York, Cleveland, Louisville, and Meridian, Mississippi, and surrounding rural areas. In New York itself we worked with young people in the deindustrialized white working-class community of Greenpoint, Brooklyn; in the Puerto Rican neighborhood of Williamsburg, Brooklyn; and in the African-American communities of Central and East Harlem.

The young people we recruited in Harlem inevitably came from some of the large public housing projects in the community, as did some of the Puerto Rican teenagers in Williamsburg. From them we learned a great deal about life in high-rise public housing. They wrote about the relative security of their homes versus the streets, about the different kinds of crews, or traveling gangs, they knew or were part of, and about the violence—even death—they must learn to skirt. Young motherhood, the temptations of drugs and sex, the value of federally sponsored employment programs, and the hope of someday making it into a productive adulthood were themes of their writing, which we wove into our book.

Partly as a result of the widespread circulation of *Growing Up Poor,* we were each invited to spend a year pursuing our research projects at the Russell Sage Foundation in Manhattan. Kornblum spent the first year there and was followed shortly afterward by Williams. Kornblum remembers particularly a seminar he attended on persistent urban poverty, which featured such national experts as David Ellwood, Christopher Jencks, Tom Cook, Faye Cook, and Eric Wanner, president of Russell Sage. Kornblum became agitated by the apparent consensus that public housing in the United States is an example of failed social policy. All the evidence for this glum conclusion seemed to come from experiences with public housing in St. Louis, Chicago, and Newark. But in truth there was little good comparative research, and no recent empirical research at all about conditions in public housing in any big city except Chicago. And even the evidence about Chicago was based mainly on two notorious projects, Cabrini-Green and Robert Taylor Homes—hardly a representative sample.

Kornblum spoke up about this lack of research on big-city public housing. His comments attracted the interest of Tom Cook and Richard Jessor, who were planning a research program on adolescence, poverty, and successful development for the MacArthur Foundation. They had read *Growing Up Poor,* and they suggested that MacArthur might be willing to support a sequel and that we come up with a research agenda on adolescence in public housing in New York City. We were delighted. The discussions led to a research program on public housing in Harlem, focusing on the lives of young people growing up there, and this became the basis of this book.

The Projects and the Harlem Writers Crew

We began this research in 1989. Terry Williams took responsibility for the day-to-day ethnographic work, which involved long hours in the projects and surrounding neighborhoods, getting to know the young people and the adults in leadership positions in their homes and other places they frequent daily. William Kornblum wrote proposals, designed research, and developed a

background of knowledge about the comparative standing of
New York public housing in the United States. He too spent time
in the neighborhoods, especially as we determined which projects to include in the study.

In cooperation with Tom Cook and Richard Jessor of the
MacArthur Foundation, we selected the four major housing projects that figure in the book. Located in Central and East (or
Spanish) Harlem, these are all high-rise apartment buildings
north of the great 96th Street class divide, the boundary separat-
ing East Harlem from the silk-stocking Upper East Side. The
projects from which we recruited the young people who speak
in this book all have approximately the same population, the
same number of low-income families, the same proportions of
young people and grandmother-headed families, and the same
typical tenant employment in hospitals and other service industries of the city. Against these similarities in demographics, we
looked at differences in the outcomes for project residents, especially children, and somewhat to our surprise, we were able
to select Harlem projects with differing rates of crime and school
failure despite the basic demographic similarities. In more tech-
nical sociological papers on the differences among the projects
we identified various features—local organization, tenant activism, cooperation between tenants and housing managers, and
recent histories of investment in a project and its surrounding
neighborhood—that seemed to account for the differences in
crime statistics, school dropout rates, and other social outcomes
of project life. But we found that no matter how effective tenants
were in organizing themselves, numerous social forces—among
them drugs, unemployment, ill health, cuts in social services—
too often negated their best efforts. In consequence, for this
book we have chosen to minimize the differences among the
projects in favor of their general contribution to a social environment which has both positive and negative features for those
who come of age among their towers.

Our previous experience developing writing groups with

teenagers brought us to create the Harlem Writers Crew. Terry Williams was the leader and primary mentor, and his example inspired the young people who appear in this book. The Writers Crew met in his Harlem apartment regularly for almost four years, and although the membership changed over time, the central figures of the book—Sheena, Marisa, Budd, Dexter, Paco—attended the groups' sessions for many months and freely contributed their ideas and excerpts from their journals. A feature of the Writers Crew that made it particularly attractive to its members was its collecting talented young people from different Harlem backgrounds. Young people who achieve in outwardly conventional directions, education and careers for example, frequently share similar home backgrounds and exposure to the thrills and dangers of street life as teenagers who are more "streety," as the neighbors put it. Dropouts and young mothers, on the other hand, who yearn to develop their talents, rarely have the chance to meet their coevals on more conventional career tracks. When raw talent is the common denominator, however, as it was in recruitment for the Writers Crew, differences in scholastic and career achievements pale in comparison with the desire to learn from others and to make some sense out of what often seems a senseless world.

Public Housing Neighborhoods

A central theme of this book is that housing projects can be good places to raise children and adolescents. They can also become centers for community building, and bases for emergency efforts to enhance children's safety. Our experience with young people in Harlem tells us that projects should be viewed as centers of neighborhood renewal, islands of hope in beleaguered urban communities. Americans are so used to stereotypes of public housing projects as drug-infested war zones that these may seem heretical notions. Empirical evidence says otherwise. Time spent with the passionate and articulate young women and men of the Writers Crew and their friends should help break down prejudices about the people who live in public housing. The projects may well be considered "high-risk" social environments for young people, because of the relative poverty of residents and high rates of drug dealing and use, of single-parent families, of early death. These risk factors, which depend in part on the sheer number of poor families concentrated in a localized area, are the consequence also of a history of neglect, and of the notion that project households do not deserve the same quality of education, health care, or neighborhood services as that afforded to more affluent neighborhoods.

We ask a number of questions in this book: To what extent do young people who grow up in high-risk environments become successful in spite of all the odds, and how do they do it? Is it easier to achieve success at the individual rather than the communal level? And fundamentally, how is success defined? Four years of research may not be sufficient to provide the most definitive answers to these and other questions, but we can offer examples and explanations from the direct experience of young people from the Harlem projects.

One finding may be stated at the outset: The Harlem projects we studied are better environments in which to raise children than the tenement neighborhoods surrounding them. Severe urban blight, addressed most effectively during the 1960s, around the time of the Harlem Youth Act, continues to ravage other parts of Harlem. During the 1980s many Harlem neighborhoods lost population and deteriorated socially and physically. Violence associated with the drug trade and with alienated youth continues to threaten residents. Rates of infant mortality and teen pregnancy, as well as homicide, rape, and other crimes, increased over the 1980s, despite major improvements during the previous two decades of social intervention.

Mention public housing and many people think: racial seg-regation, welfare dependency, a permanent underclass, neglect, violence, crack addiction, marauding adolescent "wolf packs." Whatever the case may be elsewhere, in New York City these images do not apply to most households in public housing. Yet in describing the relatively successful public housing environ-ments we have identified, we do not seek to minimize the real dangers and risks to adolescents in the areas served by public housing.

The people who live in Harlem's public housing neighbor-hoods are frustrated in their struggle to protect their children from violence, addiction, disease, and death. The risks to ado-lescents enticed by street life are greater than they have been for many years. Nonetheless, our data simply do not support the reigning stereotypes of life in public housing. Housing projects in Harlem and elsewhere in New York City are embattled, but they offer opportunities to address the threat of escalating vio-lence and murder.

Public Housing
in the United States and Harlem

Most writing about public housing is not well grounded in the realities of life in the projects or surrounding neighborhoods. Journalists are often content to offer titillating glimpses of devi-ance in troubled public housing. The photographer and sociolo-gist Camilo José Vergara, for example, has described life in the projects as "hell in a very tall place." While there are buildings and perhaps entire projects that merit this characterization, Ver-gara focuses almost exclusively on the crack epidemic in project buildings, some of which also figure in our research. James Baldwin's fierce indictment of Harlem public housing in *The Fire Next Time* (1963) speculated on what might have been if the housing had been less massive and more successfully integrated with the scale of then lively lower-rise apartment buildings. But many of those buildings are neglected or abandoned, perhaps not in Harlem's middle-class neighborhoods but in those adjacent to the projects. Better maintained and more secure than most market rentals, public housing apartments throughout New York City are filled to capacity. There is a waiting list of more than 200,000 applicants. While this does not necessarily imply that public housing is inherently more attractive than market rental, it does raise the question of what environments for child development are available and possible in existing public housing.

Existing published social scientific studies of communal life in public housing projects tend to be out of date. William Moore Jr.'s *Vertical Ghetto* (1969) and Lee Rainwater's *Behind Ghetto Walls* (1970), two of the best examples, reflect realities of midwestern public housing projects during the 1960s and 1970s. Rainwater's study, still the most carefully researched view of life in racially segregated public housing, deals with the ill-fated Pruitt Igo project in St. Louis; its subtitle, *Life in a Federal Slum,* suggests how explicitly the book explores the consequences for residents of a project that was a failure on every social dimension. Pruitt Igo was designed as a segregated community, with little connection between residential location and available jobs; that and the inadequate investment in security and commons areas earned it the poor reputation which led eventually to its intentional destruction.

William Moore Jr.'s close observation of life in another midwestern project largely supports the negative image of public housing environments found in *Behind Ghetto Walls.* At the beginning of his book, Moore presents a "soliloquy of a tenant," which could be read as an invitation to witness conditions as they are in a minority of the nation's projects:

> What is it like living in a housing project? Mister, you ain't got that much time. Besides, I got to go to the store, but if you want to walk along, I'll talk to you. . . . We have to go over to the

stairwell and walk down a flight to the elevator—it don't stop on this floor.

I hate to bring you in this stairwell with all that bad language written on the walls and all that trash and stuff piled around, but this is the only way to get to the elevator. I know you can't see where you're going too well 'cause the light's not too good but you better be careful where you step; you'd be surprised what's on these stairs sometime. Watch out for that wine bottle! Look how we have to live. That ought to tell you something. Excuse me, gentlemen, we're sorry to interrupt your game, but can we get by?

Moore agreed with other commentators of the time that the approximately 2.2 million residents of the nation's 3,500 public housing projects were living on segregated "islands of poverty." He believed he was seeing "a new matrix," one that "gave rise to our tragedy, the disadvantaged child and his new edifice of poverty, the public housing project."

More than twenty years later, the reports from midwestern big-city projects are not very different (though they are less likely to be based on firsthand knowledge). William J. Wilson notes that the Robert Taylor Homes in Chicago comprise twenty-eight sixteen-story buildings with an official population of around 20,000 and another 5,000 to 7,000 living there against regulations. Chicago Housing Authority figures reveal that 93 percent of the households are headed by a single parent and that 83 percent of nonelderly households receive Aid to Families with Dependent Children. Although it constitutes only about .5 percent of the city's total population, this racially segregated high-rise ghetto accounts for 11 percent of Chicago's murders, 9 percent of its rapes, and 10 percent of its serious assault cases. In Wilson's view, and in that of others before him, such ill-planned and ill-fated housing projects add to the great burdens on the isolated African-American and Latino poor.

We do not dispute these assessments. But again, we must

underline an alternative experience in the varied picture of life in public housing in New York City. Public housing was pioneered there; it is part of the proud if somewhat tarnished heritage of the city's social history. Some 600,000 adults and children now reside in the city's public housing, a population that would constitute the nation's nineteenth largest city. These 600,000 people represent about 20 percent of the nation's total public housing population. Among them, however, are more than 120,000 who are "doubled up" in apartments. Thus, were it not for the more than 350 projects now in existence, the city's homeless problem would be far worse than it is.

Among researchers at the federal Department of Housing and Urban Development, New York City public housing has the reputation of being better designed and constructed and in general better managed than that of most other U.S. cities. Naturally, there are critics from all ideological perspectives who dispute this claim. Some seize on that "in general," and point out that the claim of superiority does not apply equally to all the city's projects. Others argue that relative success should not be a rationale for maintaining the patterns of racial and class segregation which public housing fostered. Still others are more interested in proving that public housing stimulates isolation and long-term dependencies. However passionate these arguments, they do not recognize that there has not been enough research on public housing and the significant total public housing population in the United States to make such definitive claims.

Today there are approximately 3.5 million people living in 1.3 million public housing rental units administered by some 3,000 public housing authorities. Two-thirds of these housing units are administered by 134 large authorities, which manage more than 1,250 units each. Sixty-three percent of all public housing units are occupied by families; of the families occupying public housing, 75 percent are members of minority groups, 76 percent have a female head of household, and 59 percent receive welfare payments. In other advanced industrial nations, it is acknowledged that pure market processes will not provide adequate housing for the poor. As a result, more people live in government-subsidized housing. In France, for example, with a population about one-fifth that of the United States, more than 14 million people live in such housing. In Britain the proportion of public housing residents is even higher; during the conservative Thatcher years the reigning idea was that allowing occupants to buy their council flats would improve the public housing neighborhoods and give people a boost toward greater self-sufficiency. In the United States the idea of selling public housing apartments to "qualified" tenants is a perennial theme on the right. We will return to this issue once we have had the opportunity to see the world of Harlem public housing through the eyes of young people who live there.

The people whose stories appear in this book are referred to by pseudonyms to protect their privacy.

More is learned from the single success than from the multiple failures. A single success proves it can be done. Whatever is, is possible.

—Robert K. Merton

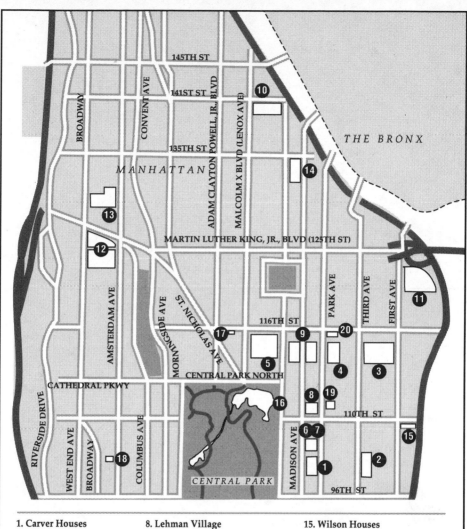

1. Carver Houses
2. Washington Houses
3. Jefferson Houses
4. Johnson Houses
5. King Towers
6. Central Park East School
7. Graffiti Hall of Fame
8. Lehman Village
9. Taft Houses
10. Harlem Houses
11. Wagner Houses
12. Grant and Morningside Houses
13. Manhattanville Houses
14. Lincoln Houses
15. Wilson Houses
16. Harlem Meer (Central Park)
17. Graham Court
   (meeting place for Writers Crew)
18. 830 Amsterdam Avenue projects
19. Clinton Houses
20. La Marqueta

Harlem

CHAPTER 1

The Kids
Uptown

*The fourth of July and all ages are engaging in firework activities.
i live in a housing project in Harlem where the noises from the pop
of firecrackers and the boom of M-80's in ash cans, sk+ [sky]
rockets launch super sparks in the sk+ creating an assortment of
rainbow colors.*

Dexter's journal (1989)

"I never want to lose my connection to the street or to the projects," Marcus Brown says. He has come back to Harlem for the summer, after leaving for the Midwest and graduate school. "What I learned about life and struggle was right here in these red-brick buildings." Marcus is now living a more middle-class life, launched, coincidentally, from the projects. But his ascending trajectory is not like that of other young people we will meet, because of his early educational experiences and certain natural gifts. The struggle is more difficult for kids like Dexter.

"Man, I've got to get out," Dexter says. "I've got to get down South or to Connecticut or someplace where I could maybe go to college. I've just got to get outta here. Yesterday I came into the building and saw some of my homeys [homeboys], you know. They be talking shit and waiting to do a deal and so on. And they're sitting on the stairs inside the building. Then, bam, two cops come up in our faces. It's like, *'Up against the wall, fast.'* I'm not holding anything or nothing like that, so I feel okay but I'm thinking, 'Oh shit, here we go again.' "

Dexter Wells, unlike Marcus Brown, longs to escape into the wider world. Dexter, who lives in a project in East Harlem, is speaking with Marcus at an informal meeting of the Harlem Writers Crew.

It's a hot summer day in Terry Williams's apartment. The Writers Crew has been meeting for a few months but remains a fresh and exciting venture. We had been thinking of such a program as a way to enhance the lives of kids in Harlem housing projects and at the same time help us gather information on adolescents in public housing. This program would, ideally, be a form of conflict resolution, countering neighborhood violence. We knew young people outside the projects who wanted to be involved and who might act as tutors. We thought that gathering a mixed group of young people would make the program worthwhile for everybody. The group from the projects should include different ethnicities and varied ages (eleven through twenty) and life experiences: teen fathers and mothers, kids in and out of school, middle-class and poor kids could make this an enterprise of living witness.

We wanted to create a forum for kids to discuss their ideas, which they would also write down. A discussion group could inform us about their aspirations and possibly lead them to contacts in a larger world where they might find jobs and use the skills learned with us. To these ends, we sought active intervention and lasting involvement. The crisis in the community in the Reagan–Bush years demanded action; so much needed to be done and so few appeared to be doing anything. There were extremely dedicated people working with kids in the neighborhoods, especially in Harlem settlement houses such as Boys Harbor and Casita Maria, but the need was still great.

Terry Williams made the Writers Group participants feel at home when they met at his apartment. He always prepared food, and had the latest magazines and other material—novels, plays, poetry; Orwell, Borges, Thomas Wolfe, and others—to read. Still he felt uncertain about what to expect at any session: so much could happen with kids bursting to talk and write. He remembers the motivation for forming the group: "I had moved to central Harlem a few years earlier, from Washington Heights. Having just completed a book about kids and cocaine in my old neighborhood, I decided something more activist-oriented would be a way to deal with the crisis emerging in my new neighborhood. The Writers Crew was my chance."

We had tried to get kids involved in writing several years before, in a project in Mississippi, Ohio, and Kentucky, and it had worked well. But this was New York City, uptown Manhattan, the projects, and there was—and is—something special about New York kids. Uptown New York kids. They are extremely savvy. Their charm and effervescence are imitated all over the world. Yes, uptown New York kids are special. They're tough and smart and resilient, cool and courageous. They come from some of the toughest neighborhoods in the country, the high-rise housing projects of Harlem.

Eighteen-year-old Sheena Taylor leaves her grandmother's apartment near 116th Street and Adam Clayton Powell, Jr., Boulevard. Sheena has been living in the projects with her grandmother all her life and wants to move into her own place soon. Brown-skinned, with auburn hair and light brown eyes, Sheena is repeatedly singled out by the boys on the block with catcalls and whistles. Looking hard but smiling when a comment strikes her as funny, she seems to enjoy the attention. She pushes her eight-month-old daughter, Xiamara, in the stroller in front of her, and raises the stroller as she reaches the curb. She crosses the street in front of the housing police station and stops at King Towers, where she leaves her baby in a nursery. Her grandmother will collect the baby after she gets off work. It's eleven o'clock when Sheena arrives at the Lehman Village projects to meet her friend Marcus, who first told her about the Writers Crew.

Marcus Brown, twenty years old, is back home in Harlem after graduating from Colgate. He lives with his mother, who has been in the projects for more than thirty years. He stands out in the neighborhood not only because of his height—he's six-five—but because of his carriage and style. He walks confidently, as if he knows where he's going. People notice his long, proud gait, and how he holds his head up and squares his shoulders. Marcus greets Sheena with a respectful but singsong "Hello, my beautiful sister." As they walk together they see Reuben, a buddy of theirs who is not meeting with the Crew today because he wants to see some old friends of his.

Of all the kids in the Writers Crew who understand street life, homeboys, and trouble, Dexter Wells knows them best. At seventeen he is on five years' probation for his arrest for activity in a street drug gang. He lives with his mother and eight-year-old brother in a small apartment in the Washington projects on Harlem's east side. Though Dexter does rap, and bears a striking resemblance to the rapper, he is no Ice Cube. He moves with a bob and weave, a gesture Ralph Ellison might call "the most elegant walk in the world." He navigates carefully to get to the meeting, avoiding projects where "beefs," or fights, might break out. He walks around the Johnson projects, although he would like to talk to Mrs. Cordero there; she said she would help him find a job with Strive, an employment agency that operates on the east side of Johnson. But that's the Puerto Rican side, and he has to steer clear of the Puerto Ricans for now. He proceeds toward the Carver projects, avoiding the Madison Avenue Robo Mobsters Crew, and then to Schomburg Plaza, where he has friends, and crosses Malcolm X Boulevard and heads toward 116th Street. No problem.

At Terry Williams's on 116th, Budd, Marisa, and other kids from the neighborhood are already seated and engaged. Two graduate students are also present: Rosa Carillo, from the City University of New York, and Ann Mische, from the New School for Social Research. These are just two of many students, journalists, writers, filmmakers, and scholars, the group will meet over the years.

Budd is sixteen and lives in the Carver projects with his mother and two sisters. He is shy, and says he came because Mrs. Montana, the tenant association president, told him he had better get his life straightened out before he kills somebody or somebody kills him. He is elegantly coiffed and wears intricate jewelry on his wrist. With him at the meeting is his friend Speedy, who is Puerto Rican; Speedy doesn't say a word. Both are members of the Madison Avenue Robo Mobsters Crew. "I want to get out of the projects," Budd says, "and get into something different." He wants to leave home because he doesn't get along with his stepfather.

Marisa, a seventeen-year-old African-American who lives in the Johnson projects with mother, father, and younger sister, is pregnant with her first child; she is expecting in two months. Her family is upset because the father is Dominican, not African-American. Marisa's interests—writing and working with young people "in constructive ways"—make her job with a local youth agency all the more rewarding. Like many in this group, she has joined because the word was out on the street that we were looking for kids who like to write. She is proud to be part of the Harlem Writers Crew.

The Meeting

Today's meeting begins to the sounds of the rap group A Tribe Called Quest. The kids' talk is momentarily lost in the sounds of

Ron Carter, the famous jazz bassist, playing on the group's latest album. One Crew member, Jack, is quick to point this out and heads for the food on the dining room table.

Dexter, sitting with the other kids, wants to talk about his troubles with the police. He knows the kids who are here for the first time will have questions. Most are in the living room but some have gathered at the dining room table.

After a few minutes, when most of the food is gone, Paco asks the inevitable newcomer's question: "What is this about?" Terry Williams tells how the Writers Crew began. He talks about public housing projects and how poorly understood they are. Instead of being considered good places to bring up children, they are often portrayed as hellholes, drug-infested jungles. The Writers Crew, Terry explains, is not only for kids from the big Harlem projects; it seeks to reach out to all young people from the neighborhood who want to write about their lives, then meet every week to discuss what they have written. Other kids from outside the Harlem projects will occasionally visit the group. Terry introduces the two graduate students, Rosa and Ann. They have been writing about their impressions of Harlem and will share them with the group. Terry also mentions that one goal of the Writers Crew is to find jobs for participants.

"Maaan, a J-O-B." Dexter spells out the word with a low moan. He has been working part-time but cannot connect with a full-time job above the minimum wage. "Now I could get down on the job thing. You know, like what I was telling before, about the other night and the cops, you know. That shit wouldn't be coming down all over us if we had jobs. If I woulda had a job I could be outta the whole scene. I mean, here are some of these fellas—like, guys I know forever, and they ain't into shit. They be playing Sega and Nintendo all day. So they're all sitting on the stairs in the projects and kinda making it hard to move up the stairs and like that. Then in comes the man, and bam, we got our faces pushed into the wall."

Masses of kids like Dexter and the others in the Crew are

growing up in the 'jects. By any conventional reckoning, Dexter, a high school dropout with an arrest record, is not a successful adolescent. But it is in the realm of the possible for him to change, given the fortitude, the occasion for second chances—which are in no way automatic—and adult help. Yet if Dexter's attempt to make a new life for himself succeeds, he will have to be considered extremely successful, to be alive and free to develop his human potential.

We can offer many examples of creative intelligence, resilience, resistance, and success among kids growing up in housing projects. And though their surroundings and eventual "success" may set them apart, young people in the projects are in many ways no different from those elsewhere in the country. Their desires are the same: a good life, safe and free of trouble, a decent job, a nice place to live. But unlike many people their age—most white teenagers, most middle- and upper-class teens—they face a constant barrage of ritual insult from adult society. Middle-class white teenagers do not have to deal with the racism, discrimination, and police harassment frequently directed toward black and Latino youth. Middle-class white kids who commit criminal offenses are often automatically accorded second chances, while blacks and Latinos are not, for the same or similar offenses. No wonder many teenagers in the projects feel that compassion fatigue has set in in the larger culture. Yet many of them realize also how much discipline is needed to contain their rage when adults in authority refuse to accept their humanity, and how that rage might be channeled in positive ways, how they and their families might unite to turn their anger outward.

The hazards are many for these kids, whether in the form of threats of physical abuse from parents and police or actual gunfire in the day or night. Yet most of them seem to cope with the uncertainties of life in the projects. Dexter's strategy for dealing with "life in the 'hood" is to accept the risks as part of everyday reality. Sheena and Marisa, however, cannot accept the dangers so easily; they worry out loud about their safety and comfort. "How can I master the situation?" Dexter says. "I can master it only by looking very, very closely at what's going on. You know how in the old cowboy movies, when the bad guys are coming to town, everything shuts down and the people all hide out? Well, that's how it is here. You got to look at the street." He reads through the physical terrain along his busy street, examining people's stances, looking for bulging waistbands (evidence of guns) and tied laces on sneakers (for quick exits). There is a psychological terrain to examine as well: "When everybody is sitting quiet and nothing is happening, no smiles, no hugging, no talking, you know there may be some tension or beef out there. But when you see people slapping palms and talking shit, things are cool."

Dexter and most other members of the Writers Crew live in buildings with interior elevators that stop at each floor. (This is unlike many notorious Chicago projects, where the elevators run in exterior shafts and skip floors; the residents often must wait for elevators exposed to the howling wind.) Interior courtyards with community gardens, playgrounds, and bench-lined sidewalks make many Harlem projects more open than most commercial developments of the same scale. All New York City projects have community centers and day-care facilities, of varying quality perhaps, but there they are. And most of the projects have active tenant associations. When Budd tells the Writers Crew that Mrs. Montana told him to go to the meeting so he could start to get his life straight, we hear the influence of a veteran tenant organizer and activist. When Dexter tells the story of his latest hassle with the police, there is a tenant association involved in his story.

"The other night," Dexter explains, "I'm coming out of my building and the kids are in the hallway. I know they're there to deal and everything like that. See, when the guys are waiting in the stairway like that, some of them don't move out the way of people who are using the stairs. Some of them are polite, they move so people can get by. Other ones get an attitude. They just act so stupid. They just stay there like fools. Now this gets people pissed. And some of the neighbors, they know what's going on in the building too. They know that there's this lady who gets high. She's become addicted to the stuff. That's how it happens. She begins to let them use her place, and they be coming and going all day. Then she shorts someone, so there's a beef. She gets hit with a pipe. I mean the shit gets so stupid, and there's all this yelling. So of course the cops are gonna come. The neighbors call them, so they know exactly what is going on and who to look for. And then there's me, trying to be clean. I'm coming down and I get caught right in the middle of this. I see the cops got these fellas. Some I know, like, they're my guys from the buildings. There's some others not from here. So I turn around and made it back to the apartment. It's not like I'm doing anything wrong, you see. It's just that who needs this shit. So this cop, he sees me turn around and he yells real loud, 'Hey, you, get back here.' But I just lock the door behind me."

The other Crew members are listening quietly, nodding now and then. This is normal for them but they are waiting to see how it ends. "Later I come down again and I'm sitting with the boys," Dexter continues, "and bam, they're back and I'm up against the wall with the others. This one cop, he's yelling at me, 'Didn't I see you before? Weren't you the guy who ran into the apartment? Where do you live? What's your address?' I tell him my address. The cops pat me down. I'm not carrying nothing. What a great feeling. Some of the fellas are acting stupid, angry, or smart. This makes the cops mad and they're screaming at them.

"The fellas, they got no ID, nothin'. Some of them don't live in the project. I try to stay cool. 'Look,' I say, 'I got ID.' I can show them my ID with the picture from the graduate school. This changes it all up. Now I'm talking to the cops, explaining shit. They let me go, but I stand around waiting. Then they let most of the other guys go too. Except the ones they already know, who are really into the shit. They take these two guys I don't know up to an apartment. Then after a while they come down with a whole safe, like that's where there's drug money stored. Now they have these kids collared."

Dexter is proud that he can speak to the police now. It has taken a long time to learn how to talk his way out of trouble. "A lot of the guys freeze up. They can't talk. It used to be they'd call you a pussy for trying to talk to the cops, but that's bullshit, really. I go ahead and talk other people out of trouble now. We just need to learn how to talk through these situations. There's too many of us been killed the other way."

This statement draws loud assent from the group. All the kids in the room have lost friends to the violence of the surrounding streets. They know how important the ability to talk is. But they also know how often even this ability can be futile against the stray bullet or the silent killer. Recently a boy was taken from a nearby playground and never seen again. The Crew members are extremely upset about this. The boy lived with his mother in one of the best tended and best organized of the major projects. Someone mentions the tragedy of Jessica Guzman, a young girl in the Bronx who was abducted and killed, allegedly by a man she knew in the neighborhood. Silence and a collective shudder takes over the group, until someone mentions having seen a child alone on a tricycle riding past a couple smoking crack.

The image brings nervous laughter to some and sad expressions to others. It is not unfamiliar. They have heard and seen everything, and they feel the need to explain: All of them are involved in some way with child care as part of their family lives. The vulnerable lone child represents a different order of problem from those they normally encounter in the projects, where there is almost a mania for watching out for children. The difference between life in the older tenement blocks and life in the projects is at once clear as far as child care is concerned. The high-rise project buildings make child surveillance much more difficult than in the lower tenements.

While parents who have the means routinely channel their children toward after-school activities of all kinds, parents in housing projects often do not enjoy such a choice. In the Harlem projects, about a third of households are receiving welfare payments, and many more are poor, without being on welfare. All the massive Harlem housing projects are home to large numbers of children; in fact, almost half of the residents of the projects are under twenty-one. In a project neighborhood of eight or ten high-rises, with a total population of 3,500, there are at least 500 girls and boys between ages ten and eighteen.

The Writers Crew members have varying sensitivities to and feelings about the problems of younger children. Sheena, a parent herself, is naturally concerned with children and child care, but many others her age are more interested in the world of teenagers and young adults. Younger children, usually siblings, often seem a burden to them, and they do not discuss them spontaneously. The situation of their own age group presses on their minds far more readily, and even heavily.

Sheena

While some Crew members brought considerable sophistication and experience with writing, others came to the group raw as far as writing was concerned, but with street experiences beyond their years. Sheena was one of the latter. Around the time she joined the Writers Crew, at eighteen, Sheena had been in the streets "playing games" for three years. "I like to hang out," she says, "and I did as much as I could. I partied."

Sheena was introduced to the Crew in the summer of 1988 by Marcus Brown, the twenty-year-old whiz kid. She was living in the Taft projects with her paternal grandmother and her baby daughter, Xiamara. Sheena's mother had died from a heroin overdose six years earlier, and Sheena saw her father only sporadically. Her grandmother, she says, "has always been there for me—I don't care how rotten I've gotten, I don't care how much trouble I've been in. We understand each other, and I love her to death."

Sheena's grandmother has lived in the projects for thirty years. She loves Sheena and wants her to avoid street life, find a positive course, and focus on Xiamara. She expresses concern for Sheena's well-being. "She needs guidance and the Writers Crew and others have done a good job, but since high school she has been mixed up with some bad elements, and that has hurt her."

The bad elements, what Sheena calls "the wrong people," were the ones with whom she would "smoke reefer, cut classes, and hang out in the halls when I could get away with it. By the time I was in my tenth year I was outta there." Leaving school gave her more time to do what she wanted, and that meant having sex with boys and getting high for fun. "I was seeing so much negative stuff around me, I didn't pay any attention to the positive things."

The turning point in Sheena's life came when she became pregnant. She wanted the baby from the start, but her boyfriend didn't. "He wanted me to have an abortion, but I was strong about this. I knew I needed to have my grandmother's blessing, because this would be her baby too in a way. You know, the best thing to ever happen to me was having this baby. I would still be hanging out on the streets somewhere or maybe have gotten myself killed if I hadn't had my baby."

Traveling Companions

Whatever direction Sheena may have found in the Writers Crew, she could not escape the hazards of the projects. Along with three other teenagers, she was arrested on drug possession charges in Suffern, outside New York City.

After her grandmother called Terry Williams to tell him the news, Sheena herself phoned him. She sounded distraught and scared as she told him, "I know this may sound weird to you, but I have just spent the night in jail with all these crazy white folk. I am so happy I didn't have my baby with me on this stupid trip with these stupid motherfuckers."

Sheena went on to tell Terry what had happened. "Listen, I went with an old boyfriend of mine, David, who I know used to deal drugs, but he told me he wasn't into that no more and was going up to Albany to see his family. He said he had some smoke [marijuana] and we could party all the way up there. All I had to do was keep them company. The 'them' was his girl-friend, a Dominican named Carmen, and another girl named Simone. We take off and get out of the city, and we're having a good time. We stopped for gas in this town and take off again. An hour into the trip and we was stopped by the police. But do you know, David didn't have no driver's license, no registration, and the damn car wasn't even his. Hello! We were fucked. So the cops took him aside and asked who we were and then separated us. Carmen, who was in the front seat, started to sweat and looked real funny. Me and Simone just kept talking to each other and waited. Then the cops, they were two white cops, asked if they could look in the trunk, and David said yes. So they did. They say they found a bullet in there that can penetrate bullet-proof vests.

"They took us to the local precinct. I don't think they found anything, they just wanted to see what we were all about. Well, Carmen started to freak. She was very nervous, and screaming about how she wasn't going to jail, and the cops told her she had nothing to worry about, since it wasn't her car. We get to the precinct and Carmen is sweating so much she faints. She just fell down in the middle of the floor. In a few minutes the police brought out a female officer to search her. She found four hundred packs of cocaine on her. Four hundred packs of cocaine! My God, I started to freak now, because this bastard David didn't say nothing to us about this and we all now involved in it."

Sheena asked Terry to write a letter in her defense to the county judge; she wanted it clear that she had nothing to do with drugs, and she wanted her participation in the Writers Crew known.

Terry Williams wrote the following letter:

The Honorable Horace Sawyer
Orange County, New York

Dear Judge Sawyer:
I am writing on behalf of Ms. Sheena Taylor, a member of the Harlem Writers Crew project. Ms. Taylor is a talented member of our team of dedicated teenagers struggling to find a better life in New York City. Ms. Taylor has been and continues to be a productive and valued member of our group and is an important link in the success of our project. She has been invited this year to Harvard University [Sheena and other members of the Crew had been asked to speak about their community], where she will be giving a talk about her role in our educational program. Ms. Taylor has the potential to be a gifted writer and is currently working on a novel for our project. I am willing to come to Orange County to speak on her behalf, and will assist in providing counsel if needed to help her in any way. She is a valuable person who deserves a second chance.

Meanwhile, Sheena was freed on her own recognizance. David, who had a rap sheet as long as a southern preacher's sermon, apparently had been using young women to transport cocaine upstate for some time. Once the letter was given to the court, Sheena said, her lawyer worked harder to resolve her case. After four appearances in court, Sheena finally saw her case dismissed. The judge wrote a letter apologizing for having her come back so many times. "The judge told me my case should have been thrown out at the beginning and I shouldn't have been called back anymore," she recounted. "You don't know how glad I am to be back in the projects. I was scared to death I might have to go to jail."

Night as Social Frontier

The presence of some five hundred teenagers, or soon-to-be teenagers, in not much more than one or two square blocks has consequences on the young people and their families that have never been very well understood. Imagine, for example, how many fast-food stores would be needed in the immediate neighborhood of a large housing project to supply even the basic jobs that give so many young people their first legitimate paychecks. Imagine how it feels to be a teenage boy among hundreds of other teenage boys when you are not six-five and a talented ball player like Marcus. Imagine how it feels when you do not stand out in anything at all, when you are surrounded by the luxury and opportunity of the most exciting city in the USA, but you and your friends don't have the money needed to go to the Village or to Times Square.

You might decide to walk downtown—except a group of uptown kids immediately draws the attention of the police and, perhaps worse, of roving posses of other kids looking to fight. So without money in your pockets, you jump the subway turnstiles or, more typically, you hang out for yet another evening, in the stairwells of the buildings if it's cold, in one of the courtyards between buildings if it's balmy, drinking a forty-ounce beer or smoking marijuana.

Night is a social frontier in the Harlem projects. Many young people, especially girls who live with their parents, are virtually prisoners in their apartments at night, so much do their parents fear what happens on the streets. Dexter reads Crew members a description of a typical night scene from his journal:

" 'The other night I saw this girl sitting in the chair. She was in between that little corridor, the first door you come through and then the next door's locked. The other girl was doing her hair. It's right in between those two doors where you got to ring the intercom. It was late. It was going to be about two o'clock. Sitting right there doing her hair. I didn't know what to do but I had to come in the door.' " Dexter clarifies that they were teenage girls and then asks: "Even though it was late, you know, what's the alternative, to be on the street and in the doorways like that? Or in hallways and alleys and shit like that?"

"What about the buildings and floors where the tenants are very strong," Terry asks, "where garbage has to be put in bags, where kids can't hang out in the hallways, where no drugs can be sold, where parents are supposed to make sure their kids are in the house. Do you see those kinds of things going on?"

"Yeah, but I don't really try to get into that yet. I understand about the garbage and no dealing drugs, but when they say no hanging out in the hallway, and then no hanging out in the street, and no hanging out in the house, where else are kids gonna go? You're throwing them out. You're just pushing them off."

The group encourages Dexter to continue reading from his journal, and he obliges them:

" 'Sometimes if I come back to my building early in the morning I see people that's been out there all night. I mean these are not only kids, there are men and women that's out there too. I guess they're enticed with the drug game too. How are you going to stop kids from getting into it when, you know, when you got older people out there doing the same thing? It might be illegal as to law, but as to really street law, it's not. It's separate.

" 'Some projects have security. They have security guards.

The intercoms are on the outside. It's like, it's almost like, if I didn't know any better I'd say, Those are for the better people. For people, we're not, like I'm not qualified to live in projects like that. And it's just that some projects are better than others.' "

These young people—who may come across as sociable and charming or shy and reluctant—are each unique. And there are differences in their circumstances as well. While Marcus, Marisa, Dexter, and Sheena all have talent, Marcus and Marisa have more opportunities to realize that talent; Dexter and Sheena must struggle, and they walk a physical and emotional tightrope. Whereas Marisa has her family and the father of her child to support her emotionally, Sheena's only true anchor is her grandmother. As talented as any of these young people might be, they all face oppositions and challenges difficult for anyone to overcome.

Dexter's last thought leaves the group with more to deal with than time allows. Night is falling in Harlem; it's nearing dinnertime. The kids exit Terry's spacious, welcoming apartment with a sense that they have succeeded in a different kind of gathering, their own seminar of the street. There will be plenty to talk about next time.

Graffiti Hall of Fame
(Photograph by Sharon Ellis)

CHAPTER 2

Building Community and Getting Respect

It takes a village to raise a child.

African proverb

The courtyards of Harlem public housing projects ring with the sounds of youth and neighborliness. A good time to watch the public life of the common areas is in midafternoon, when children and teenagers arrive home from school. Then you can witness what Jane Jacobs might have called "the children's ballet in a public housing courtyard."

On this clear day, a line of third- and fourth-graders crosses the avenue with three adult monitors. They reach a courtyard in a project, and the children are dismissed. In an instant the orderly line breaks into a joyous jumble as the children dash in different directions toward home. At a crossing near the school, a dozen or more women, some of them with strollers, stand in small clusters. The women chat among themselves, all carefully watching the stream of children departing the school. Smiles of greeting are exchanged as children zip by, and one mother after another joins her children. When a line of smaller children appears at the school door, women hurry toward them, catching hands, straightening caps, pulling pants legs down. There are shy greetings and hugs as mothers steer these neophyte students away from their classmates toward home.

One section of the project courtyard has become a circus of children's play. Balls bounce everywhere, bikes whiz by, tag games are accompanied by whistles and shouts. Girls skillfully jump rope in rhythmic cadences, while boys play catch. Kindergarten-age children are barely separated from older kids, in space and activity. At an apartment entrance across from a newly erected fence, older women stand alone or in small groups, anxiously awaiting their grandchildren's return from school. Some teenagers have positioned themselves on benches near the basketball courts, while another group of teenagers, boys and girls alike, leaves a building with smaller kids in tow. These are older siblings who take the younger ones to activities in nearby settlement houses and community centers. Everywhere one looks there are children about, and not far away adults are watching—not only mothers and grandmothers but men of the project as well, especially groundsworkers and older men, who sit in their usual corners of the courtyard. The older people know these kids; indeed, they knew many of their parents as children in the neighborhood.

"I grew up in the Amsterdam Houses, just north of El Barrio," Dr. Pedro Pedrazza recounts. "There are so many people that I came up with over twenty-five years who are still there, and there are others who have moved out, but it's amazing how much they stay in touch." Dr. Pedrazza, a strongly built, handsome Puerto Rican, has developed two innovative education programs for local students at the Casita Maria Community Services Center in the Carver projects. One involves computers and computer training, the other after-school activities, including tutoring sessions with special emphasis on science and math. Dr. Pedrazza's programs are among the fastest-growing examples of community organizing in the projects.

How tenaciously people from the projects stay in touch was brought home in stunning force for Dr. Pedrazza when tragedy struck his family. "Just a few months ago my son was murdered," he says, apparently bearing the grief well. "He was living in Jackson Heights, Queens. He was shot in the street, for no reason that we know of." He seems compelled to tell this story without burdening us with the pain of his son's death, and brings back the subject of his neighbors since childhood in the projects, who may be poor in material ways but who are rich in spirit: "We buried my son two days after the shooting. I was a basket case, couldn't call anybody for the funeral. But you know what? Over sixty people from the Amsterdam Houses who knew him and who knew me showed up at the funeral. Some people I had not seen for ten years. The word went out. They came to the funeral out of love and respect."

We met Dr. Pedrazza in 1992 at a seminar on change and continuity over the generations in East Harlem. Participating in the event were inspiring and devoted scholars who have known and written about the community since it saw its first Puerto Rican and African-American residents in the 1920s. When our turn came, we spoke about our work with the Writers Crew and our experiences with the way people in the Harlem housing projects strive to build their community despite endless difficulties and setbacks. We described the stereotyping labels of "drug infestation" and "federal slum" that pervade press accounts of life in urban housing projects. We contrasted these images with our own growing knowledge of the deep attachments many project neighbors form.

Caring communities do not come out of nowhere; they are created with effort, hard work, and dedication. "Pile so many poor families so high up in a big city like this," sighs Virginia Johnson, the no-nonsense manager of King Towers, "and it's no wonder you get all kinds of people and it's so hard to make it work. But it can and does work, with a little sweat and blood."

One of the deepest ironies of life in Harlem is that the number of people working on behalf of the community is large but the number of people who need help expands beyond their ability to succeed for more than the immediate present. The kind of people who make communities work—Virginia Johnson at King Towers; Carmen Montana, the tenant association president at Carver; and Rose Cordero, whom we will meet in the next few pages—all bear witness to a network of mutual support, a structure of adults who are not just living but also helping, because they want to, because they need to. Yet many feel they need outside support as well, to overcome the problems in their communities.

Building Moral Communities
in the Projects

As it transects Harlem, Lexington Avenue divides massive housing projects and surrounding tenement neighborhoods into the Puerto Rican east and the African-American west; it is, however, a mental rather than a strictly demographic divide. Carefully tended gardens, whimsical, spiritual *casitas,* and a few ramshackle "squats" dot the area behind the projects. In the midst of them is La Marqueta, the enclosed market that has become a neglected landmark in the neighborhood, while the streets alongside are alive with people in a true market atmosphere.

A few steps across the projects are buildings in the early stages of renovation, and two doors from there looms a church, the Primera Iglesia Hispana Metodista-Unida. Some corners and parts of interior streets are long-standing copping zones for drugs. The entire area has always been a principal place of settlement for new arrivals, now especially Mexicans, Haitians, and Africans. They come with dreams of refuge from poverty or political chaos, circumstances even worse than those they endure here.

The J. W. Johnson projects, stretching from 112th to 115th Street between Lexington and Park Avenues, is one of 360 low- and moderate-income subsidized housing projects managed by the New York City Housing Authority. To the south, on 112th Street, are Public School 101, a large gothic structure, and an abandoned lot. The more than two hundred city-owned vacant lots in East Harlem are neither city nor country spaces. Many of them serve as dump sites, home to high weeds and lost balls from the games project kids play. To prevent their use as dumps or community gardens, their owners often surround them with high fences topped with razor wire, thus giving them the appearance of stark gulags.

The people who find or create safe places for children and adolescents in the community come from churches, schools, businesses, and organizations within it. Rose Cordero is one of these people who make a difference. Though she works in the Johnson projects, she lives in the Clinton projects, where she is the tenant association president.

"I have two daughters," she says. "One is eighteen, the other twenty. Neither is married yet. One attends college, and the other is in a GED program. I've never had trouble from the older one, but I've had to push and struggle with my younger daughter. Since kindergarten my older daughter liked school, and she always excelled. My other daughter was very lazy, and her mind was always wandering."

Mrs. Cordero, who had her daughters when she was in her early thirties, has tried to pass on to them the values her mother taught her. "I taught them pride. I taught them dignity. I taught them the importance of an education so they could be whatever they wanted to be. I told them they must have a high school diploma. I taught them to be fair, to treat the other kids as they would want to be treated.

"I've lived all my life in the barrio," Mrs. Cordero says. "Right here in Spanish Harlem. And I like it. I like the access to the subway and the bus. If I want to go to Macy's or to a play on Broadway, all I gotta do is take a train or a bus. It's all right there."

Most housing projects in New York City have at least one after-school program. The young people in Mrs. Cordero's program come from the surrounding neighborhood. "We've had this program for about five years," she says. We have about a hundred kids registered, but only about thirty of them show up at any given time. A few ladies who have been trained in an educational program come to help the kids with their homework. Then there are computer and arts-and-craft classes. The kids' ages go from five to twenty-one. Most of them are black and Latino. We get no white kids."

Mrs. Cordero teaches these youngsters the same things she has taught her daughters. " 'Be fair,' I tell them. 'If you have only one piece of candy and you can't share it, then don't take it out of your pocket.' "

Like most other communities across the country, the projects have numerous temptations for young people. And it takes discipline to resist these temptations, to refuse to do drugs, to control adolescent urges for sex, to not give in to peer pressure to get into trouble. Likewise it takes discipline to control one's rage against pervasive racism in the larger society, experienced by African-Americans and Latinos on a daily basis.

There are particular temptations for girls in the projects, as Mrs. Cordero knows firsthand. "I had to put my foot down when it came to curfews. My daughters always had a curfew. No matter what their friends said, they had to be upstairs at a certain hour. I would tell them, 'While you're in my house, this is the way it's going to be. If you want to do other than what I say, then you gotta move out.' To this day they still call me 'Toughie.' "

Push-out Pressures

Some might say that parents kick their children out of the house because they are tired of taking care of them; they would like to enjoy their own time and money without the burden of children. Others point to children's disobedience. But it is more than parental selfishness or lack of filial obedience that brings parents to force their adolescent children to leave the home. Many parents feel this "pushing out" is part of the maturing process; they think they are doing a disservice to their children by allowing them to be dependent for too long.

"My life is ending and my kids' lives are just beginning," says Dexter Wells's mother, who sounds tired from working all day. "I want to enjoy the rest of my life. There is definitely a time when kids have to move out and make it on their own, and Dexter's no exception. I have been dealing with him for a long time, and he shows no respect to me. I think he should find his own way. I don't want to be mean, but he knows he has to help more."

Dexter is cramped in the tiny cinder-block-walled bedroom that he shares with a younger stepbrother; he longs for a place of his own. Not necessarily an apartment, but just somewhere he can feel independent. But how, with no money and no skills?

One of Dexter's attempts at building a "getting out" fund didn't last long. While working as a lookout for drug dealers, watching for the police, he was arrested; he got five years' probation. Dexter went to a youth counselor, landed a dishwashing job, but then quit after four weeks. When he attended his first Writers Crew meeting, he seemed distrustful; he sat in a chair with his legs toward the door and barely looked up. When he did talk, he expressed only skepticism. He said he knew of no situation in which people did something without themselves in mind. "When people do stuff, they do it for themselves. Nobody never helped me with nothin'. What you getting out of this?" Terry

Williams explained that he was writing a book about housing, and he wanted to hear from various people in the projects. Perhaps he could recommend Dexter for a job. Dexter now looked as if he felt on more even ground, and said, "Who else is wid this?"

Because of their youthful sense of invulnerability, uptown kids like Dexter are often more willing than adults to take risks. So with some hesitation and despite much remaining distrust, Dexter agreed to join the writing group, or at least to see what it was about. More often, unfortunately, the chances that come along for kids like Dexter are far less positive. If they need or want immediate cash, and are not fearful of the consequences—whether out of boldness or out of naive ignorance—they may try their hand at street drug hustles. And if, as is true in Dexter's case, they are competent in small business transactions, the cash flows into the home. Suddenly the teenager can help pay for the family's groceries, rent, clothing. In return, the stressed and often distraught parent may not ask too many questions.

This parental posture of "looking the other way" creates a curious family dynamic. Young people involved in the drug business—usually it is young men—may take the place of their parents, in the sense that they may earn more than their employed, or underemployed, parents. The balance of power in some families shifts to adolescent children. And parental inaction creates another pattern, among black families at least: about 78 percent of African-Americans living in extreme-poverty households are women. The reasons for this vary, but one of the most consistent is that black men die much younger than black women. Among all races women live longer than men, but among African-Americans this disparity begins at age nineteen; among whites, by contrast, it begins at age forty-five. Young black men like Dexter confront life-or-death situations daily in their home neighborhoods; of those who survive, some end up warehoused in prisons; others escape by joining the armed forces. They are simply not around to keep their families out of poverty.

Many parents in the projects, and even more in the older tenements, have difficulty keeping their children in safe places, but not all parents do what is necessary to create those safe environments. Those who do organize church groups, PTAs, job-training programs, and sports activities. These parents seek out educational programs or work opportunities to advance their children's prospects, and their children accordingly have a high probability of academic success and later economic achievement. "My mother," Writers Crew member Tina says, "has made sure I've gotten a head start in my life. She got me a scholarship to Dalton. She was connected to people who helped young African-American women get on the right track. She has always networked with the right people."

To Marcus, such attempts at advancement are "not about projecting an image to whites, but about laying a blueprint of reconstruction for African-Americans and Latinos." He recognizes how adults help make a difference in children's lives. Kids from around his neighborhood who have gone to college have done so because of a good family structure, and elders they can rely on. "There are black men and women who see to it that these kids find the right way. We've had some pretty good success stories. Kids from these projects have gone to North Carolina A&T, Colgate, SUNY, Cornell, Syracuse, Morehouse, St. John's. I'm not saying people don't have their problems here, but for the most part the base is strong."

Worlds of Development

A basic distinction adults in poor communities make about young people is that between "street" and "nonstreet." When a young person is said to be "street," it means he or she has been fully exposed to the often harsh morality of street culture. Many young people who do well despite their disadvantages have been sheltered from prolonged competition on the streets. This sheltering generally comes from parents, educators, community leaders, and other concerned adults who work with them in local associations.

Marisa's story is paradoxical in this regard. She was sheltered from the street, yet she got pregnant during her teens. "My parents didn't let me hang out in the street and do all the things street girls do," she says. "But I didn't get pregnant because I was some naive little girl not knowing what I was doing. I wanted to have my baby. My parents simply didn't want me to have it. They said my life would be ruined. But I wasn't living for them, I was living for myself. They wanted me to make money, money, money. I got tired of hearing about it—they were obsessed with this money stuff. I had totally different ideas." Living with her parents, though, Marisa felt she had to walk the straight and narrow in order to have any semblance of a life. "I had curfews, which I honored. I was told to make good grades, and I did. My parents wanted me to graduate, and I did. I definitely was not a street girl. I was taught not to be a street girl, because that would shame my family. I wouldn't ever want to do that."

Marisa's association with the Writers Crew led her to find another family. The kids in the Crew have learned to trust one another, to enjoy a setting where the private reflective part of their lives is taken seriously and their opinions are respected. "The purpose of the Writers Crew," Marisa says, "is for us to let other young people know that they count. A lot of young people I know feel that once you live uptown in this city you don't count anymore. So they start not to care—they don't care about the community, they don't care about school, they don't care about going to the doctor. But some of us who live above 96th Street do care, and one of the points of the Writers Crew is to let young people meet others who do care, and let them know they're not by themselves because they live uptown. I experience the negativity here in Harlem, the racism and all of that. But I try to tell my peers that there are ways out, that we are not obligated to stick to the stereotypes, that we can achieve things in life. And I try to propose ideas. That's what the Writers Crew is all about."

The kids Marisa knows straddle two worlds, one of respectability and the other disrespectability; her hope is that they will emerge respectable. Many young people who see the value of mainstreaming, of being "respectable," are, however, ambivalent: Should they follow the rules of street life, or should they conform to the codes of the white world downtown? Marcus strives to be "respectable" in both—to be successful outside his community and at the same time remain dedicated to it. The Writers Crew is one group that provides young people in his neighborhood the chance—sometimes second and third chances—to work out potential conflicts. Often these kids need repeated opportunities to convince themselves that they do possess something of value, and that even if they may have difficulty believing in themselves, someone else believes in them.

The underlying conflict is one of identity, as reflected in a statement made by Marisa. "What is expected of me? I don't even know what kind of society I live in. People think it's bad for boys—well, it's bad for girls too. This society is hostile to all people of color, to all poor people, really." Yet she and other kids persist; and they do not completely reject mainstream culture. Their rebellion, their questioning, is in fact one way in which they conform to the larger culture. They complain about parents, teachers, adults in general, but at the same time they embrace entrepreneurial and consumer culture generated by mainstream society. They play with the values of everyday life as they know it, with the hope of becoming better human beings.

Success has as many meanings in Harlem as it does anywhere else in America. Achievement in school and community, progress through education or professional training, steady employment, upward economic mobility, and formation of a family can all be seen as traditional success. Less conventionally, as in Dexter's case, success can mean simply rebounding from trouble and disappointment, defeating the failure cycle, avoiding the risks of gang membership or adolescent fatherhood, or over-coming a difficult home life, educational delay, and social fail-ure. More prescriptive, traditional achievers tend to come from families who teach them the various rules of courtesy and sensi-ble conduct outside the home. These rules are what Rose Cor-dero received from her parents, and what she has passed on, in her own way, to her daughters. "My parents didn't talk to me as much as I talk to my girls. All my parents had to do was look at me and I knew what it meant—go to bed, or go wash up, or go clean your room, or go do your homework. Not a lot of explana-tion. But I explained things to my daughters. I was more talka-tive. I used proper terminology: every body part and its function, and so on. That's the only difference between me and my par-ents. Like them, I was very strict."

Kids in Mrs. Cordero's after-school program not only are given the chance to avoid the negative influences of the streets and enjoy various activities, such as computer classes and arts and crafts. They are also taught certain life lessons. "We teach the kids patience. We teach them how to wait for their turn when they are talking with others. All this 'dissing' that goes on is about kids' not having any patience or any feeling for others. We teach these kids about brotherhood and sisterhood."

Mrs. Cordero is adamant that children respect each other, and address each other accordingly. "They don't call each other names, like 'nigger' and 'spic' and that sort of rubbish. We make the boys respect the girls when they talk and vice versa. When boys learn that women have done great things in this country, they have a different opinion about them."

Finding Safe Places

Outside the building where the after-school program is held, children sit with their mothers, grandparents, and friends on benches. Standing nearby are two men, who alternately take swigs from a paper bag, and a woman, who waves her arms in the air. The three laugh and point to a train passing on the Metro North line. "The last time I was on a train, I was headed for Poughkeepsie," says one of the men. "You ain't never been on no damn train in your life," the woman shouts. A few feet away, a man shadowboxes playfully before a toddler, who stares in fascination as the man throws punches at his invisible opponent.

In front of another building, four old men are talking; they speak Spanish. One of them throws up his hands and the others nod in affirmation. A woman comes out of the building, singing "Good Morning to You" with a Spanish accent. An elderly resi-dent of the neighborhood, Mr. Richards, relaxes on a bench nearby. He talks about a time when few African-Americans lived here.

"I came to this place in the 1930s. There was no subway and no project then, and you had different ethnic groups here. The I-talians lived by Third Avenue. The Puerto Ricans lived by Fifth Avenue. There were more Puerto Ricans in here than colored. It was way after the Puerto Ricans came that the blacks came. All the janitors were colored then. There was lots of race problems. The I-talians beat up colored. Colored was always attacked by whites who didn't want us to move in. They would throw dead cats at us and spit on us when we got near them. Colored people couldn't go into I-talian or Jewish neighborhoods. This life has changed a little bit since then, but not much."

Finding safe places has always been a concern for residents of the projects, and not only for families with small children. Mr. Richards points to a graffiti-scarred building, a "bad building" as he calls it, where drug dealing goes on. He gestures toward an empty bench where kids deal. He and several other elderly residents, aware of the activities of such buildings, often signal each other if an area is especially unsafe.

Parents, teachers, and others have similar strategies for the children of the neighborhood, as Mrs. Cordero explains. "I tell these kids not to get into elevators with people they don't know.

Regardless of whether they are black or Latino, if you don't know them don't get in. If a person looks funny or you never saw him before, don't get in the elevator with him. Wait in the lobby or whatever. The same thing goes when they get out of school or after-school. They should stay together, come straight home, call up on the intercom. The only thing is, the intercom never works. But you see, I grew up here. I know this place, I know its troubles, and I taught my daughters how to avoid them."

But not all adults or even relatives can be trusted to provide safe places for young people, so community groups must serve that function. The Writers Crew, Mrs. Cordero's after-school program, Dr. Pedrazza's Casita Maria, and others try to support kids in developing the inner discipline needed to "make it out." These groups, to which the kids feel accountable and which they don't want to let down, may stimulate them to work beyond their own expectations and never give up.

Bringing It All Together:
Aaron's Story

Aaron Sears, a twenty-year-old Writers Crew member, lives in King Towers with his grandmother and his three-year-old son, Jason. He wants to be a writer, and he is one of those rarely talked-about African-American males who is taking care of his child. On his way to a Writers Crew meeting, this studious and attentive young man crosses Malcolm X Boulevard, mumbles something to himself, scratches his head and rubs his freckled face, then writes something in the small journal he carries.

One of the more developed writers in the group, Aaron is working on an unusual, Cinderella-like story about life in the projects. At the meeting he reads from something he has written, and talks about his life in the neighborhood. Shy and sensitive, he has undergone a transformation in attitude, and involvement

in school, church, and family figures heavily in his current success.

"I've had a confusing life up to now. I was into petty crime
and stuff when I was around ten years old. I was raised to be a
good person, but I would do little bad things like steal newspa-
pers from in front of people's doors or ice cream from the store.
I thought that if I had something I wouldn't be poor. I never
wanted to be a poor person. I never really thought I was poor
until I started watching television. It was then I could see all the
things I never had. On the other hand, I took to heart the show
Good Times because the people on it kept trying."

Aaron, who wears a metal cross around his neck, says the
church kept him out of trouble. "It gave me the tap on the
shoulder I needed now and then to stay away from bad things.
If I was about to do something wrong I would say, 'Why am I
here? Why I am doing this? This is wrong.' So the church kept my
mind on jail—it's a place I don't never want to be. It gave me
better discipline not to do the things that would make me
ashamed of myself or make people feel sorry for me.

"One thing I try to remember is that if the dreams I have fall
off, I won't lose it and do something stupid. I want to be successful, but my dream is to help people whose needs are more than
mine. I mean, like the homeless people. Have you ever thought
how nobody would want to look at you if you didn't have a
house? I had a dream that I was somebody people came to for
advice. I think I've had that dream fifty times. I don't believe you
should knock down other people's dreams. You should try to
help them come true. 'Cause, you know, there are enough mor-
bid dreams going around."

Aaron acknowledges his grandmother's positive influence.
She "was the one who took me to church, and I knew right away
that it was good for me. Being there kept me calm. I would be
all worried about my friends and the street pressure, but then I
would go to church and be cooled off. My grandmother has
always been there for me and has taken the time to listen to me.

When I was younger and wanted something, she would not give it to me right away. She would give it to me when the time was right. I later learned this was so I wouldn't become spoiled and materialistic.

"I would have to tell her the truth all the time, because she told me that equaled responsibility. She wouldn't lay a hand on me when I did something bad. She would just sit me down until I told the truth. It helped me become a better person. I stayed at home a lot, and I knew one day I had to go outside. But I was worried that outside I wouldn't do the right things."

When Aaron was born, his grandmother refused to allow his sixteen-year-old mother to take him to Ohio, where she had decided to move. His grandmother feared he would grow up hardened without his father, who had gone back to the Carolinas, where "he had more kids that he didn't take care of," Aaron says. "I thought for a while that I would grow up to be like him, with many kids from many women, but my grandmother taught me super morals. Kids today have standards but no morals. Let me tell you about a fight I had with a kid in junior high school. After he clipped me [hit him by surprise], I shook his hand, told him it was a good fight, and stepped off. I don't know where that came from, but I never really wanted to fight after that. I would observe how other kids behaved and I just thought all they were trying to do was be remembered. Fights and drugs and cars and all that stuff to impress people—that's a way to be remembered. I didn't want to be remembered for beating somebody up or dealing drugs or getting some girl pregnant.

"I had sections of myself that I acted out with different people. With my friend Hank I was a word man. I would invent all these slang words. With my friend Charlene I was a class-cutter. As a matter of fact, she taught me how to cut classes. With Christopher I was a Dungeons & Dragons master. We played Dungeons & Dragons. It's a role-playing game, and it's not for the weak-minded." Aaron met kids who steered him wrong, but his grandmother and his own perseverance helped him come back from trouble. "My friend Christopher introduced me to the five-o'clock parties. These were over at one of our friends'. The parents worked the four-to-twelve shift, and so at five the party would start. Getting to the parties was a problem because I had to get past my grandma. And if I got caught, I would have to pick her mind in order to get a lighter sentence. I got tired of feeling guilty and decided I wouldn't be with people who got me into bad places. But I also learned how to be with them and not do bad things. It was hard, and it took me a long time to learn how."

When he was fourteen, Aaron recalls, he was spending perhaps too much time with his "traveling companions." This caused problems in his relationship with his girlfriend, and he tried to break up with her. "I felt I was getting too close to her, and I didn't want to get too close. I thought I'd lose her if I told her the truth, which was that I was too dull to keep. I was also intimidated at the idea of having sex. Anyway, I got over that, and sure enough, she got pregnant the next year. She took a pill to miscarry. I was there when it happened. She was getting out of the bathtub, and she started to bleed and then to cry. When I think about it, it hurts me: I wanted to cry too but guys are trained not to cry. When she started bleeding I couldn't deal with it, so I punked out. I didn't even take her to the hospital, because that feeling for her was down and I was afraid to express myself. But now I know that girls are full of emotion and if you give a girl those feelings she will give them back to you. Later, when I got the nerve to go see her, she told me how much I had hurt her, and then kicked me out of her apartment. The boys said I shouldn't sweat her, but you know boys have to be macho. They have to use girls. They are like a corporate male and a pimp all in one."

At seventeen Aaron was a father. He decided along with his grandmother to bring up the baby. And he is cautious about adding to his family. He does not want his current girlfriend to get pregnant. "I already have a son. One day we'll have a kid, but right now one's enough."

Aaron's participation in the Writers Crew is, unfortunately, short-lived. One day, after a falling-out with Sheena, he decides to leave the group. He and Sheena knew each other from the projects and it was she who suggested he join. She says he was too possessive of their relationship: "I didn't want to talk about this, but he was crazy jealous, and we just didn't get along. He wanted me to see him and not talk to any other man. I told him that was unrealistic living in the projects. Hell, it was unrealistic living anywhere."

After he has missed two Crew meetings, Aaron explains to Terry Williams why he isn't attending. "I think it's best I stay away awhile, as long as Sheena is in the Crew." He has left an indelible impression on everyone in the Crew, mainly because of his candor, which helped others express their feelings more frankly. All the kids have layers of feelings they must peel back before opening up, and although Aaron was shy and withdrawn by nature, he did not hide his sensitivity from the group. That honesty encouraged others, even the boys, who were more reluctant than the girls to admit that they had been moved by something Aaron said or did.

Sheena, a dedicated and responsible mother, says that after hearing Aaron talk about how much time he spent with his son, she felt guilty for leaving Xiamara with her grandmother longer than expected. Aaron was, and is, fastidious about his parental responsibilities, just as he recognizes how essential his grandmother is to him: "My grandmother makes all what I do in this life possible. She has helped me, scolded me, loved me, nurtured and forgiven me. No one can ask for more than that."

A "Pick-up" Group Session

A pick-up basketball game is under way in one part of the projects. Hooded sweatshirts or T-shirts, sweatpants, and Nike sneakers are the standard uniforms. A pick-up session of another type—an impromptu Writers Crew meeting—takes place on a bench nearby. The Crew members watch the game and talk of family, life, and work.

"Did you know my little brother is a wannabe Deceptor Con?" Dexter says. "Yep," he answers his own question, "he's only nine years old, and he pretends to be in a crew of kids who beat up these other kids like the Deceptor Cons are doing. At first a bunch of his friends got together and started shaking down these kids from their school, and now they just beat up these other kids for nothing."

Not along ago, rival gangs attached to different housing projects fought whenever their turf was trespassed on. But now there is a truce among the gangs, and the Deceptor Cons, a vicious gang, are recruiting teenagers from across projects. This truce recalls concessions made during the DJ battles and break-dancing challenges of the late 1970s, the heyday of Afrika Bambaataa and Zulu Nation, and the "slash wars" for the sake of art in the graffiti movement of the 1980s. Those young people on the absolute fringe who found no place for themselves in hip-hop began expressing themselves through crime. The Deceptor Cons' starting their recruitment drive in the projects is not without historical precedent.

Marisa says the kids who join this gang and others are "crazy" and have no respect for anybody.

"I would rather my brother was in jail," Sheena says, "than in that Deceptor Con shit. Dexter, why can't you talk to him?"

"I do talk to him," Dexter answers sheepishly. "But he's hardheaded."

The idea of gratuitous violence as represented by the Deceptor Cons obviously does not sit well with these members of the Crew. They recognize the absurdity of violence, and they know they cannot be totally indifferent to it. Some seek to disarm the stress and tension of the surrounding violence through positive action.

Marisa mentions a program she has been working with,

whose aim is constructive change for young people in the city. She, like others in the Crew, has a strong vision of linking her own future with that of the community. She is extremely confident about her goal, opening her own medical practice in Harlem. "I have the determination," she says, lifting her baby up from his carriage to feed him. "I have thought this thing over more than a few times in my head—what I want to do, where I want to go in my life. I'm leaving my options open should it not work out, but I know where I want to be. And I'm doing all I can do to get there. I have this fire inside me for this kind of work.

"When I really want to do something, I get this feeling inside, like there's something trying to get out. I feel like I'm pregnant with this medical thing, but it's going to take more than nine months. When I get my degree and start my own business and all that, I will be giving birth."

Just as Marisa wants to transform the world around her into a better place, Dexter too wants to change things around himself, and he is maturing in the process. He sees writing—expressing himself in prose, poetry, and rap—as a way toward positive change. "What I want to do, and I say this for true, is to help black youths, Hispanic youths, inner-city youths do better, be better, at an earlier age than when I did."

Working and Getting Work

Often between the work we would like to do, or think we would like to do, and the work we end up doing there lies a gap. This gap between dreams of self-fulfillment and the realities of earning a living are widest in communities where people have experienced a history of race, class, and gender discrimination. Harlem is one of those places. But that does not mean the stereotype about welfare and work avoidance applies in these communities, and certainly it does not in the Harlem projects. Contrary to what many who are not familiar with life in poor communities believe, most adult residents work full-time. Why, then, do they still qualify for subsidized housing? The answer lies in the type of work they do and, moreover, the low pay they earn.

Approximately 40 percent of adults below age sixty-five in Harlem housing projects are active in the labor force. For the most part this means they hold jobs. This figure is about 15 percent lower than the New York City average. About a third of Harlem project families, especially those with young children and only one parent, receive Aid to Families with Dependent Children and related transfer payments; these parents are not in the labor force. Adults with disabilities and retirees are the other groups in the projects who do not work. But most adults, as Jesse Jackson would say, catch the early bus, in a variety of jobs. The largest number work in health care, as orderlies and attendants, practical and registered nurses, home care workers, food service and laundry workers, and so on. They work in the mammoth hospitals, nursing homes, home care agencies, and elder care centers that seem to be the only "growth industry" for the inner city. Frequently their work requires them to leave their families for the evening or the graveyard shift, and evening and night workers have an especially hard time arranging child care. Many adults in the projects, particularly Puerto Ricans, cling to a diminishing number of semi-skilled factory jobs. Like any other parents at work, those from the projects think about what their children are doing, and hope that they are safe. Furthermore, these parents hope that their children will be able to find work when the time comes. The parents know they may lack the "pull" to advise their children, so they are staunch advocates of youth employment programs and other local efforts to link their children to the labor force.

Jack, who is eighteen and lives only a few blocks from Terry Williams, likes the neighborhood he grew up in. He has worked at construction jobs here and there, and is quite comfortable with the drug dealers and homeboys who have guns and the potential for violence at their fingertips. Jack has the look of a boxer: he is five-nine, broad-shouldered, with an obvious physicality, and has big hands, with short, stubby fingers; he used to play the bass. Jack doesn't take life too seriously. Like most young men his age, he likes girls, plays his music loud, and talks about sex more than he has actually experienced. He's glib, smart, and quick to laugh. He has something to say to every young woman he sees on the street. "Hey, sister," he tells one, "you have *the* most gorgeous behind I have seen in a long time. In fact, in my whole life. Look at what you got, girl. I know all yo' foo-dy must go right to yo' boo-dy." The young woman pays him no mind. He grabs his crotch. "Hey, come meet Mack, the black vagina-finder. Bitch."

Not every kid knows the kind of job he wants. Jack is one of those fortunate Harlem teenagers with limited ambition who manages to land a spectacular job; just now he is feeling good about himself. Terry Williams arranged to get him an internship with WNET, a local public television station. "I feel like real hot shit working with WNET, going out on remotes and sharing my ideas," Jack says. "What I'm doing is in high demand. I want to go as far as I can in this field, but like always there are certain obstacles that I'm being confronted with. In a strange way that motivates me more, because I know that in spite of the obstacles, I am getting more support from people who want to see me successful at something. And I know better exactly where I want to be. I love doing what I'm doing, and being totally involved in broadcasting."

In June 1989, Jack had a run-in with the police. "I had taken off from work to get my thoughts together," he remembers, "and I was going to check out a friend who lived on Convent Avenue between 128th and 129th." On the way he noticed a horde of people on 125th Street and decided to go on 126th, behind the Apollo Theatre, where he thought there would be fewer people.

But as he proceeded he saw more and more people, gathering as they might when an accident has happened. "Then I saw a group of detectives. I didn't know what was going on, and I wasn't about to find out, because I was never into that crime-scene shit, so I kept stepping toward my friend's crib [apartment]. Then a white Corsica rolls up on me and two white men get out, telling me they are 'po-lice officers,' and start frisking me. One of them said something like, 'So you left your gun home today, huh, pal?' They told me there had been a robbery in the direction I was walking from and they wanted to ask me some questions. I was very cooperative, and I told them I had no problem cooperating, because I knew I hadn't done shit. I knew they were looking for a patsy from the way they were asking me questions. They were confused about this so-called robbery. I started to get nervous. I thought the next thing they was gonna say was that I killed somebody in a robbery or threw some old lady off a roof and shit. I had all kinda stuff in my head."

The two policemen arrested Jack, for drug possession, and brought him to the local precinct. He was afraid he would be trapped in the system like so many others he had heard about. His worries were unfounded, as the case was dismissed after a lawyer friend did the legal work for him. But Jack lost his job at the television station. He was not able to keep his regular schedule because he had to appear in court and meet with his lawyer at unpredictable times, and another intern was hired in his stead. Jack had two months left in the apprentice position, which would have paid several hundred dollars a week and paved the way for other Writers Crew members.

Jack's story underlines how important it is for young people like him to have more than just one chance. Racism on the part of the police or employers who "statistically discriminate" because they do not want to hire "trouble" truncates the few opportunities that come these kids' way. Even though Jack was exonerated, the unfounded suspicions of the police entangled him unfairly and cost him what may have been the job of a lifetime. The experience hardened him, made him cynical and resentful of whites, and fostered within him a deep hatred of the police. "White folk are fucked up," he says. "And the police are the worst motherfuckers on earth. They wouldn't have treated no white kid like they treated me. And as far as WNET is concerned, they woulda stuck by a white boy if he was in my situation, because they would've automatically assumed he was innocent."

Fortunately, other kids have been more successful than Jack in getting and keeping jobs. With her grandmother's help, Sheena was employed as a home care worker for an elderly woman. Sheena is proud of the job, and happy doing it, as she tells the Crew one day. "I like to work with old people. I make about two hundred dollars a week, and that's better than welfare. At least I can save some money."

"I'm still at Youth Force," Marisa says, "but they say they having money problems, so I don't know how long it will last."

"Oh, they got money," Jack offers, "they just wanna be frontin' on y'all all the time."

"Are you still in Washington Heights?" Sheena asks.

"Yeah," Marisa answers, "but they moving into a new place in Brooklyn, starting this program to train ex-dealers to be real businessmen."

"No shit," Dexter exclaims. "How that work?"

"They ask kids who know ex-dealers to recommend them to the program, and they train them in business management and bookkeeping and all of that."

"They already know bookkeeping," Dexter says.

"Yeah," responds Marisa, "but they are not putting that knowledge to work in a legal business program. This program will really help them. I know it will, because I know Youth Force is no joke, they for real."

New York City is the economic hub of the northeastern United States, with service, retail, and wholesale trades its main industries. The kids who live in the largest city in the United

States, the third largest in the world, with one of the world's biggest labor forces, will spend much of their late adolescence and young adulthood moving in and out of that complex labor force as they struggle to define their working lives. Too many will never find work they respect or are satisfied with, because they are not prepared. Those who are left behind without high school diplomas will be deemed unemployable and may never find work in the legitimate labor market.

All the members of the Writers Crew struggle to find and keep work. Their individual experiences vary: Dexter and Paco eventually have the opportunity to get out of town to work for the National Park Service. Tina lands a job with *Paper,* a city magazine, while Joan begins what she hopes is a career as a freelance writer. Jack tries to find any work he can. But whatever their immediate employment, all look for ways to realize the dream of work that helps them grow into intelligent, caring adults. It is a great source of frustration to the older people of the projects that without outside help they have relatively little to offer younger people in this struggle. Yet here too the dedicated adults who build community in the projects are ever watchful and involved.

Mrs. Cordero's
Labor Day Festival

At the Johnson projects, autumn is approaching. The wind sweeps up fallen leaves and blows them on the grass and under the benches. Benches are taken for granted in the projects, seemingly natural features. There are no benches for tenement residents across the street, so they stand in intimate clusters, conversing, observing, coolly posing. The mere act of bench-sitting gives people in the projects a sense of comfort and tranquility, while tenement residents may look on with envy. The

Labor Day festival run by Mrs. Cordero is under way. Brightly colored balloons and ribbons adorn police barricades, and tables are set up with games and food. Children play, their parents talk, people clap, dance, and sing to music, which is everywhere—from radios of parked cars, from radios propped on windowsills, from boom boxes in the playground. A car alarm goes off, blending with the music, then stops. Teenagers hang out on benches, while nearby their younger siblings play dodge ball. A girl walks past with a bag of groceries and stops to play. From a window her mother calls out, 'Come on in here, girl,' but when she sees that her daughter is having fun, she comes out for the groceries and allows her to stay outside with her friends. Women walk by with their little ones in strollers, and street peddlers hawk ices under a bright green and red canopy. The sounds of an ice cream truck can be heard, and children run in the direction of the familiar bells. A group of parents sets up a table for a raffle, right beside a table already selling balloons with sticks attached. A fat man wearing a green cap jumps from the cab of a watermelon truck, lifts open the back door, pulls out two chairs, and places them on the sidewalk. He is now open for business. The festival continues all night; the streets in the project are never deserted.

T-shirt design drawn by Paco, from an idea of Dexter's

CHAPTER 3
———————

Life of the Mind: Culture, Rap, and School

Malcolm is proof that people can change. From my readings and listening to him, the strongest quality I can remember was his love for his people. He had hit rock bottom and been to the mountaintop. That allowed him to have compassion for all his people in between.

Marcus's journal (1989)

———————

Thinking About Life

The commercial heart of Central Harlem, 125th Street, explodes with life. This is where everyone in the community comes to shop, whether for bargain versions of the latest fashions or Afrocentric books and recordings; to see movies or live shows; to do banking and other business; or just to enjoy the energy of it all. The throngs of passersby on 125th represent every culture of the African diaspora. In the balmy spring and torpid summer months especially, the thoroughfare becomes an international bazaar. Peddlers of African art and kente cloth, Muslims selling incense and oils, African women who braid hair, Caribbean food vendors, and vendors of cheap clothing, cassettes, and batteries, far too many to make Korean store owners in the area happy.

Among the most thriving businesses on the street are the African-American booksellers, who enjoy First Amendment protection. In a market dominated by big book chains and suppliers, these street booksellers are retail entrepreneurs of African-American literature and social commentary and of new currents in Afrocentric thought. They carry on the tradition of the renowned Louis Michaux, whose 125th Street bookstore was a center for people of African descent in earlier decades. When Michaux was forced to close his store to make way for the Rockefeller State Office Building in the late 1970s (he died shortly thereafter), a chapter in Harlem's intellectual history ended.

Along with the darkened storefronts, the blank marquee of the Apollo, and other signs of community decline during the 1970s and grasping 1980s, the end of the Michaux era appeared to signify the end of independent intellectuality in Harlem. For many, the decline of the street and the loss of its intellectual landmark also seemed inevitable consequences of the flight of the black middle class and the dominance of a despairing lower class. But the profusion of writing and art among the nation's African-Americans has produced new vitality on 125th Street.

A deep vein of interest in ideas and expressions of identity in Harlem is now being mined successfully by booksellers such as Toye Washington, the energetic and articulate owner of Toye's Books, across from the Apollo Theatre. A master's student in Harlem's City College, Toye sees a steady, growing procession of Harlem teenagers and young adults who stop not only to buy her books but also to converse about current events and controversies. To linger awhile near her popular bookstall is to hear an extemporaneous seminar of black thought.

The latest books by Alice Walker and Toni Morrison, the relative merits of Shelby Steele and Cornel West are routine subjects. And while conversations on literary subjects might occur similarly on the Upper West Side or in the East Village, they are especially vivid in Harlem as a new generation of educated—and self-educated—Harlemites emerges.

Perhaps too many people accept the monopoly that schools and universities hold over what is recognized as legitimate intellectual life. The memory of grappling with received wisdom makes it difficult to admit that people without conventional credentials can share a world of ideas and find delight in expressions of their joys and fears, whether in poetry, prose, or other articulation. African-Americans are foremost among those whose intellectual lives are often denied. Their ability to think is often considered stunted if they do not bow to the authority of the classroom and attain the salvation of the degree.

The Harlem Writers Crew, for one, demonstrates the opposite: Even in their great diversity, uptown kids are thinking, feeling, resourceful young people. The less educated among them deal all the time with intellectual problems, just as the more educated deal with the same life-or-death questions as confront their peers with fewer credentials. The consciousness of all these young people is shaped by their encounters with the city, by their largely negative experiences with school, and by the legacies of racism. Their community may be confined to Harlem, and their immediate neighborhood limited to a single high-rise project, yet the moral and intellectual quality of their experiences in these locales is far from stunting. This is particularly so when more universal meanings of these experiences can be drawn out, as they are in such forums as the Writers Crew.

The uptown kids live a half-hour subway ride from one of the world's most important cultural centers. This has always been an irony of life in Harlem, and it escapes no one in the community. Furthermore, there is a world beyond the segregated confines of the community that displays an endless craving for the culture uptown people produce. Surprisingly, teenagers are the major producers of that current cultural product. This fact tells us we have to look afresh at our traditional concepts of intellect and academic success if we are to see the true value of what the uptown kids are thinking, saying, doing, and creating.

The midtown business world has always sought ways to take uptown culture for as little money as possible and transform it into commercial culture in all its forms, which today is one of the nation's major exports. In New York City there are more culture-making and -selling enterprises, more museums and galleries, more television production offices, more theaters, more publishing houses, more fashion studios, more advertising agencies, and just more movers and shakers of culture than probably in all other cities of the United States combined, with the exception of Los Angeles.

In New York, as in many another city that specializes in the production of culture, the wellsprings and the profit centers for that production are worlds apart. An old story perhaps, but it must be told all the same: The mining of creativity from the streets of Harlem for mass production, packaging, and shipment around the world has never ceased. In fact, it has only increased in importance and scope. A tradition that started even before Fats Waller began virtually giving away songs in Tin Pan Alley— to buy a meal or a drink or put together an alimony payment— has continued with the promotion of break dancing, street rap, and hip-hop into commodities on the world market.

Why Harlem? There are, after all, other centers of popular culture, other communities where the poor gather and entertain themselves with variations of their own culture. But Harlem has always, in its own fashion, and by crossing over, produced world culture. Crossovers are an essential part of the seemingly endless stream of expressive styles that have arisen out of the experience of life in Harlem.

Where European Jew and Italian and African-American first lived more or less as equals and so were exposed to one another's culture, there was a synthesis between European popular music and the jazz and blues of original geniuses such as Louis Armstrong and James P. Johnson.

The music of Duke Ellington, George Gershwin, and Fats Waller reflects the complexity of cultural crossovers during the jazz age. But jazz music was only the beginning. Afro-Cuban music, rhumba, cha-cha, merengue, pachanga, and salsa are all examples of crossover music that, though born elsewhere, developed further in music and dance halls of Harlem and became another of New York City's important cultural exports. Bill "Bojangles" Robinson and Sandman Sims brought tap and jazz dancing to the forefront in the 1930s and 1940s, and such hip-hop tappers as Savion Glover and Herbin Van Cayseele are doing it today.

Harlem is of course not the only community responsible for the crossover music known as rock and roll. But the fusion of street-corner singing by Italians along East 116th Street with the soulful a capella sounds of African-Americans along West 116th with the muted clave beat of Harlem Puerto Ricans and Cubans contributed mightily to this brand of popular music.

Young people from all classes and backgrounds who have grown up during the eighties and nineties seem especially confused about the future. They see many adults around them full of doubt, as they are just as uncertain about how society is changing and what their place in it might be. The term they often use to describe their state is "clueless." On the other hand, many of these young people feel a solidarity with their peers, and view themselves as part of a world-culture generation. World culture and world peoples have become the major topics, indeed major fashions, for them. They are fascinated with world culture, and adore talking about related trends and controversies. But cultural movements that excite the passions of young people historically tend to be taboo in their schools, and too often these subjects are given little if any respect.

The problem is partly generational, since it is hard for older teachers to have interest in popular culture that did not accompany their own youth. In addition, since the jazz age at least, each successive generation's popular culture has sought new ways to shock the parents and their beleaguered representatives in the schools. Yet the greater anger and desperation in much of today's popular youth culture frightens many adults, especially teachers, and so the gulf between young people and educators widens. Uptown kids experience moral dilemmas on their own terms, with their own cultural references. The mental struggle, the soul-searching, the talk go on, though they are often hidden from others. Behind the booming shouts of the rap artist and the seemingly obtuse stance of a kid with his pants sliding off his hips and his hat turned awry there is usually a mind dealing with tormented thoughts and deep passions and the irresistible love of life.

Too many of the schools the uptown kids attend are deadening places in their experience. It has long been fashionable to trash the public schools. Schemes about choice in private education and exhortations for discipline and traditional values abound as pundits cluck over the schools' failure to reach young people in Harlem and other segregated American communities. The shelves of college libraries overflow with critiques and prescriptions, and yet progress is painfully slow. When the Writers Crew members lose themselves in a debate or become riveted on the feelings expressed in a piece of writing, a question always lurks: Why doesn't this happen when they're in school?

The future of New York City rests on its maintaining its position as a financial, cultural, and media giant. This means investment in higher-quality schools for all children who live there, including the current younger generation of African-Americans and Latinos in housing projects and the surrounding communities. Investment in the schools guarantees the city the intellectual capital necessary for preserving and fostering its leading position in the world. New York communities such as Harlem offer the city one of its most precious gifts: its youth.

Schools and Higher Learning

"West Side Outreach, what we call the Annex, is the school where they send the dropouts," Dexter comments one day, about a year after joining the Writers Crew. He is struggling to finish a general equivalency degree program, for which he reports to the third floor of a Manhattan high school with other dropouts and suspended students. He calls the school "Annex" because it seems only vaguely attached to the real school on the floors below. There are dedicated, hardworking teachers in the program, Dexter allows, but there is also a sense of failure pervading the students' thoughts. "It's like a convention of people who ain't gonna make it. You should see the gold on everybody. You could round up so many drug dealers there it ain't funny." Why are drug dealers there, one might ask; they have a livelihood, albeit a risky one. Dexter says that "they're used to going to school. Maybe they ain't ready in their hearts to quit, even if school don't mean shit to them. And then there's judges and moms that are pushing them. It's be there, or else."

Dexter tries to pay attention to his schoolwork, but he feels ever more thwarted by his classes. One day a girl he is flirting with, whom he has never seen before, tells him she will be at the school for only a few days while she waits out a suspension; then she will return to her regular school. "See"—Dexter shrugs— "Annex is where they send kids who are being punished."

Dexter found school a punishment already at an early age. In third or fourth grade he was at only a beginning level of reading and writing skills, and he felt intense frustration. This is the pattern of many children in his world. There is a gap between the level at which they are expected to be performing and the level at which they do perform, and the problem worsens as they grow older, until they are tempted to quit school as soon as they are of legal age to do so. Many reasons have been cited for this pattern of failure, but the truth is rather simple: Most children who do well in school come from homes in which their parents are educated and communicate expectations, monitor schoolwork, offer help, provide a daily stream of vocabulary, and participate in school activities.

School quality and teacher efforts matter too, but nothing counts as heavily as home training and home culture. Where these are limited or missing because parents are preoccupied with just making ends meet, schools need extra resources. Schools in Harlem and elsewhere require lower student-teacher ratios, more enriching activities and programs, higher expectations, and much more. Instead such resources and initiatives typically go to students in affluent communities who already enjoy advantages at home. Harlem students, Dexter and Sheena for example, must face large classes; tired, stressed teachers; few special programs or activities; and a looming sense of failure.

It is true that gifted Harlem children enjoy an advantage over children in other racially segregated communities of the city because they are combed over more closely for talent at an early age. There are numerous predominantly white schools with resources to offer. Scholarship and special assistance allow selected minority students to attend elite private schools such as Dalton, Walden, and Manhattan Country Day School. Catholic schools also offer scholarships and an alternative to public schools. And the public schools themselves, especially in East Harlem, boast some of the nation's most celebrated educational programs. But even with this burgeoning educational opportunity and choice, the demand for better and safer schools far outweighs the supply.

The varying academic experiences of Writing Crew members might be seen as representative of young people throughout Harlem. Four members—Joyce, Paco, Marcus, and Tina—won scholarships to private or prep schools. This gave them a definite advantage on the path toward educational success, but it also left them with a classic split life, with friends in the projects and different friends in school. Marcus was tapped for his academic and physical capabilities at the end of junior high, while most of the others have gone through ordinary public schools. Sheena, Dexter, and Budd are dropouts who are painfully, fitfully fighting their way back into the formal education system. Their reasons for dropping out vary: Dexter, as we have seen, is a bright kid with limited educational support at home. His spiral into school failure began early. Sheena left school because, she says, it was too dangerous: "I figured I might as well get my GED somewhere else. I couldn't concentrate. There was an arsonist at my school, and somebody set off bombs there. One day this boy was shot to death right near me. I got blood all on my jacket. I had enough. I left. And I got pregnant the next year and didn't go back."

As a result of participation in the Writers Crew, Dexter sees educational possibilities that he didn't see before. He didn't care about school in the past because he felt it as an obligation— going to school was what he was supposed to do. "I cared more about making money and rapping than I did about school. School didn't mean nothing to me. When I got out of junior high I got picked for Mabel Dean Bacon High, and so I went there. I was told I had to go, so I went. I was told to finish high school, finish college, get a job, have a family, and die. I was following that point of view. I was doing what I was told. I didn't necessarily wanna do it."

Some other Crew members who are in public school cannot wait to experience the larger world outside Harlem. As elsewhere, the kids who "make it" in the most conventional ways, despite all the odds, are special individuals. They also tend to come from families who struggle to teach them "the right way." And they may be motivated to do better by the grim aspects of life in their challenging neighborhoods. Yet the plight of those they may leave behind may cause them anguish. This conflict between mobility and loyalty to origins is common to many coming of age in poor communities.

Marcus, who speaks for many of his Harlem peers, knows this conflict well: "I always remember hearing, 'Don't forget where you came from.' I know people who should remember but don't." And as a twenty-year-old private college student, primed for a good career, he has not forgotten. "I was born in the Bronx. The place to be, right?" Marcus's parents were teenagers when he was born, and he was brought up by his great-grandmother. While his parents were in the Nation of Islam, his great-grandmother leaned toward the traditional black church. "From the time I was seven days old I was in her care. She was, without a doubt, the greatest person I've ever known. She was born in Richmond, Virginia, in 1909. In 1985, my senior year in high school, she passed away. She missed my graduation. The most important thing was her influence during my formative years, and the pervasiveness and effectiveness of her memory. I am hard-pressed to remember anything negative."

Marcus acknowledges further some "extraspecial teachers. Their emphasis was on teaching the history of people of color." Many public school teachers, he says, do not know much about the history and culture of their students, and their historical experience in this country. And many teachers are alienated from their students; they finish with classes and then go home. "Teachers don't love the children in the schools," he says flatly. "They pay close attention to some kids, and ignore the others."

But Marcus remembers his mentors. "They were very important. They gave me blueprints. In fourth grade, I had a teacher named Shirley Graham DaBenny. She had great love for her students, and she was sharp. There was no half-steppin' in her class. Mrs. D had us in check. Part of it was fear, but most of it was respect." Marcus's class included "intellectually gifted children" from fourth and fifth grades. "It was a very productive environment," he says, and the class achieved results beyond all expectations. Yet for Marcus personally it was "a wild year, being in a class with fifth-graders. I had started the year before in second grade, then finished the year in third. Then I changed schools and went to fourth. It was like I went from second to fifth grade in one year. Changing classes broke me up with my crew, and with Mike, my best friend at the time. We were together for first and second grade, and we were the smartest kids in our class, or at least we got the best grades. I've learned that smarts and grades don't always go together. When I moved up, I was in another league—I was like a rookie having to guard Michael Jordan in the first game.

"Mrs. D died over the summer during childbirth. Our class was crushed. Fifth grade was a waste—I don't remember one positive thing from that year. Mrs. D named her son after me. I've only met him once or twice, and I don't have contact with her family. I guess her memory is one thing that has kept me in the straight and narrow, for the most part. She was a beautiful sister. She was balanced and focused. She was one hell of a mentor. She still is, she's with me now."

Marcus has committed to paper some of his thoughts about community. He reads them to Terry Williams one day in the projects. "I was born out of a spirit of hope that refuses to be bound by despair. It is a spirit of hope that creates a better reality for all who come in contact with it. That is real. I was born out of the power of this spirit. So now we see there are some serious contradictions in our community. The projects are not our community. They are vertical plantations. I guess the biggest contradiction is that people we most easily recognize as successful are the ones who are the least help or use to their people."

We survey the scene in the community before us: A child drives a small toy jeep on the sidewalk. Two girls in bomber jackets walk by. A teenager supervises a kickball game among younger kids. A lone white man stands near a cluster of evergreens, frozen for a moment, talking to a youngster. He digs in his pockets for money, gives it to the boy, receives a packet, and walks toward Fifth Avenue. He glances nervously over his shoulder before jumping in a taxi and heading downtown.

Sheena: Near the Bottom

Sheena has worry all over her face. "My personal life ain't shit right now," she says. "Men suck. And when I see all these drug addicts, it makes me think about my mother. She had her drug problems, and I wonder why she was an addict. Will I be one too?"

It is hard for Sheena to remain motivated to get her GED. "I'm struggling in school. When I was in fifth grade, at Catholic school, I had a really good teacher, who would see me and always hope the best for me. She was my favorite teacher. I loved her." But Sheena's experiences after that were far from positive, and so she dropped out.

Sheena and others like her have an uphill struggle with those teachers who don't seem to care. Students who receive support at home, whether in doing schoolwork or overcoming academic frustrations, can more easily withstand a bad relationship with a teacher. But whether they receive that support or not, young people desperately crave teachers who can appreciate them, their language, humor, and warmth, and who can discipline them from within their world. These teachers who care are in short supply, and their attention is precious.

Our society offers little or no credit for "underground," informal seminars, such as those held in Terry Williams's living room or on benches in the projects. A society with a limited definition of "intellect" often denies the mental capacity and emotional sensitivity of people who do not conform and stay on the traditional track. Conventional educators' ideas about young people, which sometimes are overtly racist and demeaning, reflect the gulf between white classroom talk and fervent expressions of another style of life. Educational gatekeepers often find uninformed and unintelligent the language kids use—" 's up," "word," "yo," "sis," "bro," "chill"—and so that language and the related emotions, longings, and sense of crisis that the kids feel are often lost in the imposed structure of the classroom. The cultural gap widens. Thirty students and more in a classroom with one embattled teacher hardly means individual attention, or the opportunity to talk and be heard. So kids talk at informal discussion groups meeting in settlement houses or churches, or in places of peace, zones where no violence, in any form, is tolerated, and where the kids themselves are in control.

The Place of Peace

"The place of peace is where we go to chill out," Budd says, pulling up the collar of his jacket. "We smoke blunts [marijuana cigarettes rolled inside Phillies Blunt cigar leaves], drink forties [forty-ounce beers or malt liquors], and just hang out." The places of peace are the projects' version of suburban tree houses, nooks and crannies where kids avoid adult supervision. "We have places of peace all over the 'jects," Budd says, " 'cause if we wanna be by ourselves this is the place to be. We talk, do rap, we in-tel-lec-tu-al-ize." It's a place where kids can do what they want, without having grown-ups impose their rules. When one kid says to another, "I'll be at the place of peace," the other kid knows what's meant. Often adult tenants know young people congregate in their buildings, but they do not complain if they feel the gatherings are harmless and involve kids from the buildings, not from outside. In many instances, however, the places of peace are secret—hidden corners, secluded spots behind buildings, rooftop hideouts. These secret locations are frequently temporary, renewed on a weekly basis.

Dexter remembers sitting in a place of peace after one of his friends had just been killed and another shot in the foot by a cab driver when they ran away without paying the fare. Dexter didn't go there to smoke or drink, he says, but "just to chill out, to think about life." Thinking about life—and about death too—that is what goes on in the places of peace. Thinking and talking—about dreams and visions, and about the evil and stupidity in the world. Dexter needed a place to contemplate: Why did these brash friends of his, buddies since kindergarten, foolishly run from a cab? Why did they take a cab in the first place, if they had no money?

Who would suspect that young people are contemplating and conversing so intensely, all over the projects? The stranger walking late on a blustery night along upper Madison Avenue might see only the shadowy figure darting here or there, or the lone lookout, shoulders hunched up against the cold, lingering on a corner. But in scores of stairwells and basement passageways teenagers and young adults sit engrossed in passionate talk of life and death, sneakers and jewelry, rap and graffiti (and the qualities of each that make it art), the subways, military squads and hit men, nationalism and religion—and other subjects far too many people imagine these young people do not care about or cannot articulate.

In the places of peace the kids do not gather in gangs, but still many people will see them as outlaws: after all, they are not doing anything "constructive" by smoking pot or writing on walls. To be young and poor is to be considered an outlaw. This is true not only for kids in the Harlem projects, but for most working-class youth in urban America. In the old deindustrialized white communities of New York—Greenpoint, Maspeth, and Bay Ridge, for example—there are well-known parks and passageways where teenagers and young adults gather, not in recognized gangs but in groups that only verge on respectability.

The physical features of the community establish the boundaries of the social universe for project kids during their early years. In Harlem, various groups divide the territory: among them, Puerto Ricans maintain niches, larger than the places of peace, on the east side of Fifth Avenue, and Dominicans do likewise on the west. These areas, including parks and street corners that are highly valued real estate, are commonly the source, and the arena, for disputes between groups. Abandoned buildings, as well as renovated ones with new tenants, also can be the source of conflict between groups vying for territory or for control of a specific drug market.

The projects, which too often are viewed as dangerous places within the city, to be avoided at all costs, are themselves like small cities. Many adolescents feel trapped there, although some find the hope and courage to overcome that feeling. They are encouraged by individuals and organizations in the community, people who seek to steer youngsters in productive ways. Still, many youngsters struggle through adolescence. Marisa and Budd learned how to maneuver around the city early, but Dexter and Sheena, who live within commuting distance of one of the world's most concentrated and expansive labor markets, have not taken advantage of such an opportunity because they are poor kids, with limited resources and few adults to help them.

Odd jobs, intermittent work details, stints in summer job programs, and some steadier work—in supermarkets, for small offices or messenger companies—provide some project kids with their first paychecks. In some white working-class communities, the gap between adults and teenagers is even wider than in Harlem. Kids in these communities may become involved in more self-destructive behaviors, more use of (heavier) drugs and alcohol, more irrational crime, than kids in the Harlem housing projects. But black or white, all are outlaws to some degree, because they are in the limbo between childhood and adulthood, with limited rights, uncharted futures, little privacy, no legal places of their own, few possessions, and an attraction to adult behaviors that for them entail violating the law.

The Block

Terry Williams happens to meet Dexter near his block one morn-ing before a Writers Crew session. Dexter has left his journal at home and wants to return to get it. On the way he tells Terry about activity on the street. "The Puerto Rican niggers got the crack," he says. "The black niggers got the coke." The word "nigger" bothers Terry, and he asks Dexter what the word means to him and why he uses it. "Yeah, I know what it mean, but it don't mean what it used to mean. Anybody can be a nigger if they shit is raggedy." Terry leaves it at that and lets Dexter continue.

"Some of the kids have gotten more and more out of con-trol in the 'hood, man. They are really outta control. The black kids and the Puerto Rican kids are out here battling over bullshit. Now, I never really spoke to them Puerto Rican niggers because they be on some exclusive tip. You understand what I'm say-ing?" Terry does not. "Listen, they girls be they girls and shit, you know. And they don't really wanna fuck wid us. That's how I see it. And they start bringing in that drug shit is like extra head-aches. Now, I used to come out here all the time. I would be standing here chillin'."

Dexter squats, takes a penny in his hand, flips it as he looks down the street. He tosses the penny high in the air, misses it. Lets it roll. "I wanna go to school real bad, away from here. I gotta get outta here because of the kinda shit that's jumping off right here on this block. I know people hustling and coming back and forth here. I be standing right here and I be saying, 'What's up? What's up?' Whatever, whatever. But when I feel it's getting too hot, I'm outta here, because I ain't got shit to do wid it, and I damn sho' ain't going down for nothing I ain't getting a cut out of. So the Puerto Rican nigger, boom. One day I peeped [saw] the Puerto Rican niggers. I'm cool with them. But gradu-ally the black kids routed them niggers [Puerto Ricans]. Now, you know, we used to be out there, but we don't really have much to do with each other. Of course we say 'What's up?' nowadays, but that took a couple of months.

"Then one day we in the chicken joint, right? Now, the other black kids with the coke, they fucking with the Puerto Ricans. They be talking with them, whatever, you know, kickin' it [laughing and joking] with them, smoking blunts, whatever, whatever. But I used to hang out with the black kids, not the Puerto Rican kids. So one day the Puerto Rican kids say something to me and we kickin' it and we was cool, boom. And then I started hanging out with them. Don't you know the next fucking day they wanna break out some kinda Puerto Rican–black war. The first question I had was, Why? At what point did this situation escalate to this?

"Well, it's because they opened up that fucking game room. Let me tell you, that joint is a murder zone. I can't be in that, man. You see, if you have a beef [a dispute between rivals often leading to gun play] with somebody and you in there, a nigger sees you up in there, they run up on you, they shoot everybody in there. So listen, this one black kid on the block, he be standing in front of my building, and I say to him, 'What's up?' I see him all the time. This day there was mad customers coming up to me as soon as I leave my building. They think I'm dealing 'cause I'm out there. So I go to the game room and find this kid and I tell him, boom. 'Yo, you better step to your business, because there's money out there for you.' And he say, 'Yeah, here,' and gives me the game because he was playing pool. So he left, boom. I shot around for a little while, I really don't play, I just wanna get off the street to avoid these motherfuckers asking me for shit I ain't got, and don't really wanna get wid this. Not really."

Dexter catches his breath, then continues. "I leave after the kid comes back and I'm on my way back upstairs and I see mad niggers fighting in the street. It's this one Puerto Rican kid with his face all bleeding and shit, and this black kid who is taller and heavier than the Puerto Rican kid. Then it got all hectic. He [the Puerto Rican] looked bad even though he was beating the black kid up at the time. But the Puerto Rican was bleeding, and you know, if you bleeding you look like you got the worse of things. 'Cause, you know, niggers is there, bitches is there, and that's what's really escalating the shit. And after this is over they announce a beef, and a few days later the kid I went to tell about the customers, he had a cousin that just got outta jail, and the Puerto Ricans ran up on him and shot him.

"They didn't kill him but they shot him. I heard two versions of the story. From the blacks I heard that the cousin was tussling with the gun after the Puerto Ricans rolled up on him, the gun went off, and he was hit. Boom. Now, I know the Puerto Ricans, right? And I'm kickin' it with them and they say somebody got shot, blah, blah, blah, not much detail. So, check it out.

"There's two people that see everything in the street: the smoke man and the crossing guard. Hey, the smoke man is like a fucking newspaper reporter and the crossing guard is like Connie Chung. They blow Channel Four outta the box. They know all kinda shit. So the smoke man tell me the Puerto Ricans run up on him and *took* the gun from him and shot him. The crossing guard say the same thing. But the fucked-up part is, even though they didn't kill him somebody is gonna die, because the black kids gonna respond and you know the shit ain't over. I mean, this is on both sides of town. If it ain't downtown, it's uptown. It's just mad shit going on, and I'm trying to get outta here as soon as possible."

In the weeks that followed, Dexter tried to bring the two groups together in a kind of truce. There is no general pattern of black and Puerto Rican hostility in the community, but in the hustling zones where buyers converge from all over Manhattan, any division among street peddlers becomes a cause of violence. Eventually Dexter's peacemaking efforts failed. Soon another young man was shot down on the corner in front of a grocery.

Small wonder that gangster rap is born here, in these neighborhoods where violence is perpetuated at times brother against brother, sister against sister. The true enemy is lost in the quest to find some meaning in life and a crumb from the table of an oblivious democracy.

Only a very small proportion of the Harlem housing project population is involved in the kinds of violence Dexter describes. Most of the street hustlers, adults or teens, live in the impoverished old tenements and decaying walk-ups surrounding the better-organized projects. But the inevitability of the violence weighs heavily on all residents of the community.

Much of street culture is an expression of anger, defiance, and contrariness. The street has been a place to avoid, a place where bad company lurks, where you learn a lesson, where the sucker punch is perfected, where cursing is elevated to an art form. No good, or at least rarely any good, comes from the street. A good girl is one who stays off the streets; a bad boy is one who stays in them. The street represents an untamed immorality that not even the church can convert. Middle-class blacks avoid it, and decent poorer blacks try to shield their children from it, knowing full well, however, that one or two might end up there for a time, take their hard knocks, and then climb out into respectability.

In the past, the no-good men who stood on street corners cursed the saints, stabbed the sinners, fought the police, were in and out of jail, and lived in fear of no one. They were the "crazy niggers" white men feared and sensible blacks dared not confront. And likewise today: Boys out of reform school or the county jail or the local hospital, holding a switchblade with one hand, their crotch with the other, their attitude "Don' fuck wid me"—this is what street culture is all about.

The street has, it is true, given rise to more positive elements. The dozens were born in the street, the blues raised there, and jazz mythologized. Shine, the fictional black character who survived the sinking of the *Titanic,* and Dolomite, the prince of raunch, originated on the street. Doo-wop singers and music hustlers with processed hair and fat blondes and Cadillacs come from the street, and comedians such as Moms Mabley, Pig Meat Markham, Redd Foxx, and Richard Pryor have carried this tradition to stage and screen. But the street has spawned other, more infamous institutions—numbers rackets, pimping, extortion, drugs—and so has come to embody the nonconformist, antisocial—indeed, antipolice and antigovernment—culture of refusal, a world of coolness and confrontation and "Nothing is sacred." Yet there are rules to obey on the street, and only by following them—or being smart or lucky—does one survive or escape the street. "Never fall victim to the street con of fetish money," one street hustler commands. "Listen to the wisdom of street elders. Do what they say, not what they do," says another. "Never discipline yourself by the street codes, but by the workingman's day," is another one's wisdom. But it is difficult for most project kids to follow these rules, to remain on the street, maintain self-discipline, and stay out of trouble.

Just as crucial as the street in the life of adolescents in the projects are changes in the greater society, the neighborhood, the family. Disruptions in the national and world economies send shock waves to poor project communities, where marginal employment is the norm and what is a "mild recession" elsewhere is a "mild depression." These economic reverberations are lasting, and their effects will be felt in the twenty-first century, and certainly by young people. What is remarkable about project communities is how young people can resist defeat, when assisted by caring adults and their own intelligence and coping strategies. Positive values imparted in the home and the neighborhood give special impetus to these young people. The idea of their being members of a permanent underclass becomes doubtful; at best the term is a dangerous catchall, which misses the intelligence, resourcefulness, and rebounding energy found in poor communities. Many youngsters—including those in the Writers Crew—have demonstrated their resistance to defeat by not accepting their "underclass" condition, by striving for excellence, trying to be the best they can be.

Cultural expressions such as hip-hop are responses to the constancy of racism and oppression. They are the creative ways to work out, or restructure, anger and aggression. One can only imagine what social benefits could result if young people in poor communities had the opportunity to develop their full potential under less stressful conditions.

Byword of the Uptown Kids
(from a T-shirt)

CHAPTER 4

Rap and the Coca-Cola Culture

As I submit these words into my journal I'm pumping shit with the Jungle Brothers and we kicking about the perserverance of Be-bop and the whole scene of where and how rap is the heir.

Jack's journal

"**W**hite folk want you to believe that what they promote is really what rap and hip-hop is all about, and that just ain't so," Marisa is saying. "It's like I wanna avoid a culture that produces Coca-Cola because it ain't the real thing, it's the inauthentic thing. It has not been real since they took the cocaine out of it." The Writers Crew is discussing matters of culture and authenticity, but inevitably the conversation turns to rap. In a group of uptown kids with varying levels of education, rap is a subject with appeal for all. Everyone has opinions about the racial and moral aspects of the rap scene, especially in Harlem. But even in this community the young people have plenty to learn about the meanings and origins of their culture.

Marisa talks about a world rap conference sponsored by the

French consulate, which she, Terry Williams, and others attended at the Apollo Theatre a few weeks ago. She mentions that
one speaker focused on gangster, or hard-core, rap. This speaker
attempted to explain the cultural role of gangster rap by apply-
ing the ideas of the French psychiatrist Frantz Fanon. His psy-
choanalytical interpretation of racism and colonialism,
considered revolutionary in the 1950s and during the French-
Algerian War, might be relevant to racism in the United States
today and to the feeling many black American teenagers have of
being "internal colonials" in their own communities, and ultimately relevant in understanding the desperate origins of rap
lyrics.

The Crew members are confused: Who is this Frantz Fanon?
What does this all mean? Terry Williams tries to clarify. In *The
Wretched of the Earth,* a book written in the 1960s, Fanon ob-
served how the Algerians faced daily acts of heartless repression
during the war with France. Famine, eviction, unemployment—
these were daily realities, and it was no wonder that many of
them turned to violence. In their frustration and anger, some
Algerians turned that violence against each other. Gangs
roamed the streets; people killed each other for a pittance. The
native, as Fanon saw things, might fear even his fellow citizen as
much as he feared the enemy, the foreign colonizer.

The kids in the Crew call forth similar acts of aggression in
Harlem, South-Central LA, and Philly. They are familiar with
gang violence, if only indirectly, and they can understand somewhat better now the relevance of Fanon in their own world. They
are like the natives, neglected or rejected by the colonizers,
whose world they might aspire to. They live in a state of constant
tension.

Jack brings the topic back to rap. "I know for sure that
hard-core and gangster rap is what the rappers nowadays is all
about," he states with authority. "But I think brothers and sisters
have much to work out for themselves before they go blaming
the settlers." Sheena—who also attended the conference and
who is curious about why the French are so interested in her

culture—admits to liking the beat of rap music but fears that "most of this gangster rap hurts relations between black men and black women."

"It's threatening," Jack allows. People are "scared of what rap and hip-hop will do to white youth. I think they worried about white youth agreeing with N.W.A. [Niggers with Attitude, a California-based rap group] about fucking da po-lice. Down with the system as we know it. They don't want another sixties on their hands. So they try and shut these rappers up. White kids are being lied to, too. They wanna hear the truth like black kids."

Behind this talk of rap and hip-hop, however, are the more basic subjects of black culture: how it is produced; what symbols and language are used, what stories told, what rituals performed; what world-views emerge; how this cultural capital is preserved. One of the most important questions the Crew deals with is how black culture both expresses and shapes young people's strategies in navigating their world. They repeatedly discuss how they can resist defeat by "talking back" to the larger culture, through art, about racism, oppression, and statistical discrimination.

For some of the kids, these are abstract topics. Many aspects of black culture in the United States have been declared off-limits to them, unfit for them to know about. They may learn that American popular culture borrowed from the field chants of slaves, that jazz had its origins in African drumming, and that the blues are derived in part from Negro spirituals. But they are not taught about far raunchier—and therefore banned—forms of expression that come from the same old folk forms.

In studying the origins of gangster rap, one must consider the dramatic accounts of the violent lives of bad "street niggers," such forbidden characters as Shine, Dolomite, Stagger Lee, the Voodoo Queen, Dirty Nell. These and hundreds of other mythical heroes and antiheroes populate the improvised poems and slick monologues passed from one generation to another in the "joint."

Dolomite is a mythical bad-ass, but more than that, he's a

bad nigger. He's the opposite of John Henry, the black paragon who shot his bolt in the service of rail magnates. "Dolomite gives shit out," it is said. "Others take it in like wash or dick." The Writers Crew hears a version of a prison rap, or "toast," about Dolomite recorded by folklorist Bruce Jackson:

> Some folks say that Willie Green
> was the baddest motherfucker the world ever seen.
> But I want you to light up a joint
> and take a real good shit and screw your wig on tight,
> And let me tell you about the little bad motherfucker called
>   Dolomite.
>
> Now Dolomite was from San Antone,
> a rambling skipfucker from the day he was born.
> Why, the day he was dropped from his mammy's ass,
> he slapped his pappy's face
> and said, "From now on, cocksucker, I'm running this
>   place."
>
> At the age of one he was drinkin' whiskey and gin,
> at the age of two he was eatin' the bottles it came in.
> Now Dolomite had an uncle named Sudden Death,
> killed a dozen bad men from the smell of his breath. . . .

In the literature of prisons and migrant camps and street corners, men with nothing find power in words. A man will recite into his and other jail cells as interminable days go by, and in his narrative, bad tough guys like Dolomite and Stagger Lee seem to conquer all obstacles with fist and penis. By the end of the toast, however, it is clear that the bad tough guys are alone and unfulfilled. Dolomite, for instance, after going to Africa, where he gets a job "kickin' lions in their ass just to stay in shape," and getting "kicked out of South America for fucking steers," is said to have "fucked a she-elephant till she broke down in tears." And, finally his "roll was called":

> They had his funeral, carried him down to the graveyard.
> Dolomite was dead but his dick was still hard.
> The preacher said, "Ashes to ashes, dust to dust,"
> said, "I'm glad this here bad motherfucker called Dolomite
>   is no longer with us."

There is a grim clarity in Dolomite's epitaph. But not all characters in the forbidden folklore of isolated black men are violent bad niggers.

The African trickster is transmogrified in the United States into a slick pimp who with his verbal ability and cunning conquers men and especially women. Shine uses his wit, his mouth, and his speed to ward off danger and escape from difficult situations. In one of the most famous prison toasts, the wily Shine finds himself the only black on the ill-fated maiden voyage of the *Titanic*. Shine himself brings the captain news of the disaster: "Up stepped a black man from the deck below . . . hollerin', 'Captain, Captain, don't you know, / there's forty feet of water on the boiler room floor.' " Disregarding the bad news from a lowly black, the captain tells Shine: "Go back, you dirty black / we got a thousand pumps to keep this water back." This is one time, Shine decides, that coldhearted whites will not have the better of him. In a flash he jumps overboard, "waves his ass, begins to swim, with a thousand millionaires lookin' at him." The daughter of one of the millionaires comes up on deck, with "her drawers around her neck" and "nips on her titties sweet as plums"; she offers this and more if Shine will save her. His mind on survival, he shouts back to her, "A nickel is a nickel, a dime is a dime / get your motherfuckin' ass over the side and swim like mine." Finally, having evaded sharks, and the pleas of sinking Wall Street brokers, Shine reaches the shores of New York: "When the news got around the world that the great *Titanic* had sunk, / Shine was in Harlem, on 125th Street, damn near drunk."

Today's gangster rappers spin violent yarns in which they blast their male opponents and conquer the "bitches" in their lives. Many of their images and scenarios are derived from older "underground" oral traditions such as men's prison poetry. These chanted improvisations, old and new, are a way of releasing anger. But a major difference between the older poetry and the newer commercial rap, aside from the latter's use of musical sampling and driving rhythms, is that the older poetry was never intended for audiences mixed in race, class, or most of all, gender.

Black entertainers such as Moms Mabley, Redd Foxx, and Bessie Smith borrowed liberally from forbidden cultural forms and brought them into the smoky roadhouses and "buckets of blood" where black working-class folk took their pleasure in the late hours after work. In the angry nineties, where to shock the sensibilities of a paying audience one may feel the need to evoke the most bizarre sins of the flesh and to celebrate the most violent acts possible, outrageous male fantasies become veins of profit for the commercial culture. In the process, weighty moral and cultural issues are raised publicly, on a scale rarely experienced.

The Writers Crew discussed at length the controversy over rap culture. One image that rap pushes in people's faces, in a way the underground poetry never could, is that of women as sexual objects. Black prison folk poetry is by men deprived of any immediate possibility of sustained relationships with women. Their hang-ups about women, and their envy of black women's possibly greater acceptance and claim to exist in white society, are buried deep in their ritual forms of expression. But in rap these dilemmas of black life are exposed commercially to a vast public, and they deeply trouble young people, especially those who are most sympathetic and desirous of knowing their origins.

Joyce believes that "sexism and racism are twin heads of

the same beast," and that men are afraid or reluctant to discuss "the gender dope." She wonders about how readily many young people "look to nineteen-year-olds for political ideas. Think about it: These rappers are young kids. Theirs should not be the last word on sex, politics, or war."

Jack finds it "absurd that people take hip-hop so seriously. We forget about the humor and the fact that much of hip-hop is about fun and making fun."

"I don't think it's so much fun to be called 'ho,' 'gangster bitch,' and all of that," Sheena responds. "Dr. Dre had that album out a few years ago about how a girl should suck his dick. That was fucked up, not funny."

"Y'all just don't have no sense of humor," Jack says. "Joyce, I know you take shit way too seriously, but I'm surprised at you, Sheena. You got it going on, when it comes to the fun part. What's up with this overly serious shit?"

"It ain't about being overly serious," Sheena counters. "I just have an opinion about the type of rap that I have a problem with."

"I think girls be on a mission for equality in society," Dexter suggests. "One of the biggest problems for black men, for black people, is females and males. Yo-Yo is cool, but she joined this all-woman group. Salt 'N' Pepa [female rappers] did a video about women not being barefoot and pregnant. They on an equality trip. They have the men in the aprons. In that song called 'Sensitivity,' they be saying something like, 'I need a man with a big cash flow, if he show me his paper [money] he's good to go.' Even my girl is on an equality trip."

In many ways Dexter is closest to the street world of the lonely men who never had relationships with their fathers and resented, for more reasons than they could ever account for, their seemingly powerful mothers. If we reflect back to the compositions of street folklorists and prison poets, a recurrent fear is that of being "pussy-whipped." Dexter is very quick to fear the tug of the apron strings. At first it is painfully difficult for him to consider the young women's viewpoints. How can he deal with these opposing claims and not change his own attitude and behavior? In time, however, he comes to see the female perspective. This continuing dialogue across the gender divide will prove to be one of the most significant achievements of the Writers Crew.

Rap and the Projects

Whatever its unacknowledged debts to underworld male folk poetry, rap has more recent influences as well. Jack seems especially familiar with them. A few years older than some of the Crew members, he feels he's been around long enough to hold forth: "Most of y'all may not have heard of Afrika Bambaataa and SoulSonic Force, the Cold Crush Brothers, or DJ Breakout. You might remember Grand Master Flash but I bet y'all don't know the Jamaican, Kool DJ Herc, or Spoony Gee. Or places like El Que, or Roof Top, Danceteria, or the Roxy. These places and these cats were around the industry when the thing was just starting to jump off and nobody got paid. This was before Def Jam and Tommy Boy records and all of that. Nobody knew what to do with this shit, and a few people got rich because they knew how to count the money, but most middle-class niggers dissed rap as too street.

"When Sugar Hill Gang came out, the number-one DJ in project land was Bambaataa, who was head of Zulu Nation, the largest crew in the city. Kid Capri today is nothing compared to Bambaataa then, who controlled kids all over the five boroughs. They will tell you that when he came out with the record 'Planet Rock,' Tommy Boy records was nothing. *Noth*-ing. This is history, y'all better dig that jazz."

Bambaataa and his group, SoulSonic Force, played an important role in the development of hip-hop because they brought kids together at a time when gang warfare was subsiding but could have easily slipped back into all-out war between black and Latino kids from Manhattan and gangs from the Bronx. Bambaataa traversed the city, rapping, playing music, and making peace among teenagers. He was a street disc jockey with an increasingly respectable reputation, and when he spun records on a turntable, he created a special sound. Teenagers loved it. He made appearances at high schools, parks, and clubs throughout the city. It was the role of the disc jockey as cultural hero that made hip-hop's popularity grow.

Bambaataa, Grand Master Flash, Kool DJ Herc, and other street disc jockeys influenced radio disc jockeys, who in turn began giving rap a wider audience. Disc jockeys became the creative force behind hip-hop. Clubs used them to encourage people to enter and throng on the dance floor, moving to a new beat once they got inside. A club DJ would maintain a continuous beat, without even a break to change records.

But there was a permissible "break" in the hip-hop ritual, a pause with a purpose, which allowed for a drum solo and a dance—a break dance—while the DJ made a cut between repeat bars on dual turntables. Break dancing became the craze among former gang members, who were now calling themselves crews (groups organized to make money) and performing the less violent ritual of break dancing against rivals. Rival gangs would come together on a street and, instead of fighting with guns, knives, sticks, and bottles, would try to outperform each other's improvised moves.

Madison Avenue's exploitation of hip-hop dancing was not as forthcoming as its appropriation of hip-hop music. Recordings were the logical and most exploitable cultural commodity. Rap music was in. The examples of Bambaataa, Grand Master Flash and the Furious Five, and other unofficial ambassadors for peace showed teenagers the possibilities for expressing themselves, and perhaps making money and gaining fame—and in a positive, legal, "good" way. Much of the gang warfare changed from violent confrontation to creative competition. This is not to suggest that Afrika Bambaataa and Grand Master Flash had *the* decisive hand in the control of youth gangs, but they arrived on the scene when gang warfare was declining and many gang members were looking for new, positive activities. While the influence of Bambaataa's interest in the Muslim religion held many potential gang members in check, some formed crews whose activities were not so much dancing or rapping, as drug dealing and boostering, or shoplifting. And others attempted to gain fame in another field entirely: graffiti.

Graffiti crews were a natural offshoot of the rappers and dancers. Hip-hop became a cultural movement with rap music at the top, break dancing in the center, and graffiti at the bottom. These artistic expressions took different directions as they were auctioned off to the highest bidder from downtown, who evaluated which could be exploited best, with the least effort, for the biggest profit. Graffiti was immediately out of the question: the distinction between art and crime was too blurred; graffiti was an unpoliceable phenomenon.

Paco, one of the first hip-hop artists, did break dancing in clubs, wrote rap lyrics, and tried his hand at subway graffiti and T-shirt art. He comes from an artistic family; his father is an architect and his mother a free-lance photographer. They separated when he was eight. Paco has had problems with his mother and stepfather, and he left New York to study in Ohio, at the Columbus College of Art and Design. He has always been interested in different forms of artistic expression. "I never wanted to limit myself to just one type of art. I like painting. I like drawing. I like film and I like train graffiti."

As a child Paco modeled for fashion magazines. "I did that stuff because my mom made me do it," he says. "I didn't know any better. But when I got a little older I knew I wanted to dance, and break dancing was out so I started to do that." Paco toured the country and Europe with a break-dance troupe.

Paco and Dexter have collaborated on a few projects. They have designed Afrocentric puzzles, and a T-shirt for Underground Intelligence, a reach-out program for young people in Harlem that seeks to bring them together and realize that street culture is an inherent part of their legacy and should not be made invisible. The T-shirt shows a manhole cover, pushed aside, the dark hole below. A hand extends upward holding the edge of the hole, while another pushes the cover back. Paco explains: "It's like we're underground and trying to come out. We're emerging as artists, powerful forces of black consciousness in the world."

▬▬▬▬

Creative Invisibility

Adolescents the world over often feel insignificant, invisible, and want to break out of that feeling, even if they have to make an outrageous statement. For some Crew members this is a familiar topic of discussion. In the 1980s, Paco remembers, he was writing subway graffiti at age twelve. "I was a toy writer then. I just wanted to sign my name, give the city my autograph. I wanted to make a name for myself." For him and others, however, graffiti grew to something beyond just the art of the autograph. "We weren't interested in just signing our names. All of us in my crew were into being full artists. We were all going to art school and were not like most of the other kids, who had no training.

"You know who is up now in the projects and everywhere uptown is this kid Blone. His rep is based on how many people recognize his tag. He has a certain style that goes with that tag, and if he can keep getting up all over the place he'll get fame. And fame is what everybody wants."

There are at least four types of graffiti in project neighborhoods that may generate fame: Tagging, signing one's "tag," or identifier (usually not one's real name); students learning how to write, or toy writers, engage in this. "Bubble up" writing, so called because of the bubbled effect on letters, numbers, and figures; this is still done by older writers who have not gained fame but who remain masters of New York graffiti art. Wall writing, which involves covering entire building walls, often with memorials to dead teenagers or celebrations of notable personages. Piece (short for "masterpiece") writing, which entails creating large three-dimensional works and which is the most advanced version of the art form. The Graffiti Hall of Fame, located on 106th Street and Park Avenue, offers some of the most prominent examples of New York City graffiti art.

Adolescents in Harlem have learned from the world around them how important it is to control one's own destiny. They recognize, in the development of drug crews for example, how important it is to be the boss. They have seen heroes rise and fall, not just in movies and on television but in real life as well, and they understand they have to do for themselves: advertise for themselves, provide their own publicity, be their own agents in a cutthroat world. They are skeptical and resentful of many adults, who, they feel, have betrayed them and continue to do so.

Writers of graffiti and hip-hop artists challenge adults by creating provocative accounts of the adolescent world, by starting their own record labels, and by attempting in the process to lay claim to the urban environment and make society take notice of their existence as people. They rebel against the imposed environment by picking new surfaces on which to inscribe their identity, or by improvising lyrics that question existing values and contest for the minds of the young.

Many people view graffiti as desecration of property, vandalism. To them, a building with graffiti is a building with problems. As a matter of fact, graffiti is one of the first signs that a building is going "down," say many tenants and tenant leaders. But young people such as Paco see graffiti as art, and not necessarily good or bad. To Paco, tagging is "a good way to express art. But people see it as bad and vandalism."

Graffiti is not only art, but crime, play, expression, and invention. A developmental approach is needed if we are to understand it as art and crime, and see it from the point of view of project kids. Many graffiti artists begin tagging, scribbling their names on public surfaces, around the age of twelve or thirteen; they continue this social ritual for three or four years. In their mid-to-late teens, they do "bubble up" writing, and in their late teens, three-dimensional piecing. Three or four years of "active" writing on public surfaces affords a rebellious, daring apprenticeship, where the act is everything: working the craft, developing a "hand." It is this apprenticeship that is most misunderstood and viewed as vandalism by the larger public. Many graffiti writers really want to write, and many have emerged as stellar artists, selling their works for tens of thousands of dollars. Early graffiti artists—Lady Pink, Daze, Futura 2000, Crash, Lee—have had their works shown in galleries in New York's SoHo, and their fame and fortune are what graffiti artists in the projects are striving toward. Graffiti is culture capital in its infancy.

Meanwhile, most project residents see graffiti as a reason buildings are perceived as dysfunctional. "It only takes one bad apple to make a building bad," says Carmen Montana. "It takes much more effort to keep a building good. You need to organize everybody to keep a building good, but just one kid from one family can make all the other families look like they don't care about where they live. One child with a marker can make the building bad."

Graffiti, like so much else viewed as negative, is in reality a positive response to invisibility. Parents and others who pay no attention to kids get graffiti-riddled walls. Teachers who refer to their students as animals get kids who leave school early, feeling alienated and disrespected. Social workers who claim that kids won't change will see no change. An economy that does not provide jobs for young people gets drug dealers who try to make money any way they can. Anger and a fascination with urban life create graffiti as both art and crime. Hip-hop is all one motion of energy. Teenagers in project neighborhoods struggle to find a place for their energy. And through hip-hop and related forms the creative intelligence of adolescents is channeling this energy for good. Although Paco was one of the first teens to explore hip-hop in its various forms, he is but one of thousands whose commercial career never blossomed. He is an ardent critic of whites who have suddenly discovered hip-hop, and an unofficial guardian of the culture. But hip-hop is a learned art form, and although African-Americans and Latinos are its progenitors, they cannot possess it in totality.

At a Crew meeting, Joyce expresses the desire to record and thereby preserve hip-hop culture in writing. She and others—among them Nelson George of Public Enemy, Greg Tate from *The Village Voice,* Havelock Nelson, and Michael Gonzales—are defining the culture for its creators. The Crew discusses "Love's Gonna Get You," a song by the rapper KRS-One. Its lyrics tell how a youth, frustrated by the lack of opportunity in the job market and the lack of cultural identity in school, and attracted by the promise of quick money, cars, and condos, is swept up into the drug trade, fast-paced violence, and eventually jail. The moral of the story, as KRS-One says, is that you can get hurt by too great an attachment to material wealth.

The group listens intently to words by Paco inspired by KRS-One's rap song:

My mother is struggling,
to make ends meet.
My father hasn't worked
for the past few weeks.
The man ain't lazy,
he just got caught out there,
laid off from a job,
you know that shit's unfair.
I always feel

I have to eat every meal
whether I'm hungry or not.
I know the deal,
food is minimal.
In my crib that typ-i-cal shrinking,
having meat is like myth-i-cal thinking.
At the table into a trance, a dreamlike state,
a gaze, wondering about the good old days,
when things will be different,
as they need to be,
like the white folk eatin' steak on the color TV.

Sheena doesn't like much of the song because it reminds her of her brother's situation: he is on probation for dealing drugs. "Listen," she tells the others, "I know Dexter told you what our argument was about when it came to that song." Dexter looks over as if to say, "What argument?" "But," Sheena continues, "for those of you who missed it, we'll re-create it right here. Right, Dexter? Me and Dexter had argued back and forth about when KRS-One says that the cash is good, everything's chill, he'll get himself a gun and his brother a piece—and then asks what did you expect to go down. And I felt like he shouldn't have made a song like that, because my brother and kids like him listen to these rappers and do that shit.

"My brother and his friends are only fifteen and sixteen, and they don't understand like we do about this stuff. They feel like it's okay to sell drugs, get guns, and all of that. They say, 'See, the rap song says so-and-so.' And I know it wasn't meant like that. They interpret it like that because as poor kids they feel they need to sell drugs to get where they want to go. And if they get busted, then they just say, 'What the fuck am I supposed to do?' I told my brother what the song was really saying, but he just said I was crazy and didn't know what I was talking about."

Paco mimics Ice Cube's rap with one of his own: "I don't wanna work, / struggle to be somethin', / do my best, get paid less, and wind up wid nothin'./ With all the effort / and nothin' to show, / in this crazy world I just wanna grow / and get the proof / for the effort I've made. / To put it simply, I wanna get paid."

"We ain't talking about that, Paco, so why don't you just shut up for a minute?" Sheena tells him.

"I thought the song was real," Dexter says smiling, "but I told Sheena what her brother is doing is what is available to him to make some money and not what this damn record say. KRS-One is telling the story from the street. This is street word and when he say, What am I supposed to do, he means it, because that's the way the kids out there see it. They gotta buy sneakers and jeans and have no money, so what are they supposed to do?"

"Yeah," Paco jumps in, "but in reality these kids know they have to deal to make money because they don't have no other way to get the sneakers and all the gear. KRS-One didn't create that situation. KRS-One is just a songwriter and an entertainer. A good, powerful one but an entertainer just the same."

Moved by the personal issues the lyrics raise for him, Dexter tells the group about how at a critical time in his life he began to feel a "switch," as he calls it. "I got tired of doing what others were telling me I should do. I decided at seventeen that I was gonna do what *I* wanted to do."

It was through writing and rhyming—which sometimes took the form of boasting—that Dexter made his "switch." "I used to write my rhymes for the crowd. There wasn't no real message in what I was saying. I was doing what I had heard others do. Everybody told me I could rhyme and I believed I could, so I did. I was writing for a purpose, but I wasn't sure what the purpose was. I had to go through this switch thing first, to realize why I was writing and had this deep interest to write. So when I made that transition, I wasn't writing about girls, partying, drinking, smoking, fighting, and all of that anymore. When I switched, I started writing about how I really see society, and how it is."

Sheena says, "I know I was put here for a great purpose. Maybe I will reach that purpose one day. But I've known since I was a little girl that I was put here for something really special. I've always said to my grandmother that God wants me to do something real good in this life. And she told me I would always be good."

Paco, on the other hand, says his life was guided for him but he didn't know what leads to take. He knows there is a purpose to his life, although he is unsure what it is right now. "I see myself ten years from now and I figure all the gifts that I have will have been put to the test and realized. Right now, I'm not in any position to talk about being established or anything like that. Hell, I'm still looking for a decent job. I know I want to be in graphic arts, but I don't know where or what that will be. There are lots of things I am capable of doing. I just got to find the one that will get me established or at least on the road to a profession."

As these young people make their transitions they struggle to find confirmation in themselves, in role models, in friends and lovers, in their own creative work, in their families and communities. They see rap as their generation's contribution to the generation of a world culture. Their sense of closeness to and possession of rap and its producers, as well as their emotional and intellectual responses to rap, are among the strongest feelings in their lives at this time. No wonder they react so forcefully to the way rap seems to be taken from them by the white culture industry.

Hip-hop and White Boys

Hip-hop and white boys, culture kleptomania and cultural possessiveness: all the Crew members have something to say on this. Marisa argues that "culture vultures" who exploit black culture do so because there is "so little of value in white American culture to exploit." She asks Terry Williams what he thinks, and he tells her he has come to understand that the core of the art form is threatened by the commercial establishment, because the real producers of hip-hop have little or no control over their product. In a Coca-Cola culture, each new homogenized product—Vanilla Ice, New Kids on the Block, Marky Mark, to name only three—hides the true form behind a screen of imitation.

Marisa agrees. The record companies, she says, release only "music that isn't threatening. That's why you see Vanilla Ice and Marky Mark and all the phony talk about violence, because the real get-down artists are almost never given airplay. They be underground and still manage to sell millions of records. Look at *Fear of a Black Planet,* or even Ice Cube's record *Amerikkka's Most Wanted.* They [record companies] only want people to dance, and not listen to what the artists are saying."

Jack insists that people should listen to the latest hip-hop transformation: jazz hip-hop, performed by such groups as A Tribe Called Quest and Digable Planets.

Joyce describes this music further: "It's real mellow, smooth, and the torn acoustic base is so good. But I'm afraid it's not gonna get the groups financially what they deserve. I think the latest Tribe Called Quest album might sell less than their last one. And that album sold 290,000. It might sell 200,000 in New York, and I don't know how it's gonna do in the Midwest. You see, because this is not like the Bonita Applebaum album that got them so much airplay. This one is not going to generate that kind of radio play. It's really hard, because with this bad pop-rap like Vanilla Ice and Geraldo [a Latino rapper] and this gangster rap like N.W.A. flooding the market, it becomes hard for other rappers to come out and make music. It's really great music, but they can't get the support of the record companies because they are not pulling in the dollars."

Paco wonders aloud: "When are these rappers gonna stop sampling everybody's shit and do their own stuff through and through?"

Before he can say another word, Jack puts on a tape of the group A Tribe Called Quest, which is progressing into jazz hip-hop.

Joyce resumes talking about the Tribe album, and about how Tribe and the Jungle Brothers and other groups show their Afrocentricity. "Every other word," she says, "runs like Af-ro-cen-tric, da da da." On the album, she points out, a singer "goes back to a jazz base. You know, he starts out making that parallel between his father and himself and hip-hop with bebop and strings it along with sort of a jazz base and riff and drumbeat, then takes it back to references of Africa, and he's talking like groovin'. And this one line about Africa goes around and then back around with like hip-hop and then takes you to the Last Poets with that sample and ends it there. And what's really soft in what he's saying underneath all of that is excursions, excursions. It's gorgeous. And it's the kind of album in its simplicity there is like so much there. And it kills me because it's just not going to sell like it's supposed to."

"They'll get paid, though," Jack says with confidence, which is based more on hope than reality because, as Joyce has made clear, record companies are interested not in cultural aesthetics or improving the race through Afrocentricity, but in money.

Joyce, the budding professional music critic, shifts the attention to the split in audiences. "New York audiences tend to judge rap by New York audience standards. And I would have to say, probably with a whole lot of bias, that we have really good discriminating values when it comes to rap. But that does not mean it sells across the rest of the country. What sells across the country is either gangster-ghetto shoot-'em-up stuff or that real pop stuff with just riffs." She maintains there is great pressure on record companies to record music that will receive radio play. "It doesn't matter how good it is in terms of quality, as long as it's at the top of the charts. And that mentality dictates what gonna have to be put on the market."

Paco mentions that he went to school with a white kid named George, who is a member of a nationally known break-dancing group that Paco also belonged to before it became commercially successful. When he was a member, Paco and others in the group helped teach Mikhail Baryshnikov and Twyla Tharp how to break dance. He now dismisses George—who goes by the professional name Search—and white boys like him as "culture vultures." He and Search used to be "like best buddies," but there was too much competition. "He learned how to boogie from me. I used to boogie first, right? Then I got the scholarship and he couldn't deal." And, Paco says, Search "used to think he was black and shit. He had an identity problem. When we would hang out, people would think he was Puerto Rican. So he would play like he was Puerto Rican. And that's an identity thing.

"There's a whole bunch of white boys out there copycattin'. Like P. Nice, he's at Columbia now, I think." But Paco admits he still admires P. Nice's talent.

Joyce disagrees. "P. Nice is nothing but a white boy from Columbia. His connection to the music is an aesthetic one. Search sees his relationship as a cultural one. But P. Nice reads James Joyce and Gogol and he's very much a Columbia English major. And that's what I dug about him. When he gets out his gear that's who he is."

"But what *is* his gear?" Paco says. "I'll tell you what it is, it's a cane, a suit, a cigar, and he walks around looking like some pimp out of Brooklyn. Look how he's portraying black people. Here he is, some English major at Columbia doing this shit, pretending to be black, and yet that look is nothing like him. It's wrong."

Joyce raises her hands for emphasis, "But Paco, as much as we want to be culturally possessive of the music, hip-hop is a learned art form. It ain't been passed along in your genes be-

cause you happen to be African-American. Now, Vanilla Ice has
no right to be out there. Search calls him a rapist of the culture
because he has never spent a day in the [African-American]
community. Search was at El Que. He was at the Roof Top. You
know what I'm saying. You have to pay a price." Even though he
is a "white boy," Joyce says, Search is "good people" because
he has frequented the rap underground. "He's not a vulture, who
reduces African-American culture to mere style. It's not like you
can just flick on a TV and gather all the jewels of the culture and
never have to experience anything." And while that, she says, is
what Vanilla Ice and others have done, it is not what Search and
Third Base do. "I understand about being culturally possessive
about this music, especially when it's exploited. But Search and
P. Nice were there and they know more about hip-hop than
many of the black kids I talk to, whose connection to the music
started with Public Enemy."

"Even if I accept all of that, P. Nice is still phony to me,"
Paco says. "I do see a difference between him and Vanilla Ice,
and I wouldn't compare the two, but he is phony in his own
right. Especially since he is this Columbia English major and all
of that, and he gets up on stage and tries to play it like he's
something else."

"Most rappers and other performers do that," Joyce points
out. "They have different personalities for onstage and off. But
if he tried to do that lyrically, I would have a problem with it."

"But he tries to sound hard," Paco says.

"Yeah, so what? He can," Joyce responds. She mentions the
rapper Ice Cube, "one of the gentlest, most softspoken people
I've ever met. But on recording and onstage that's not what he
gives off at all. You know that if P. Nice sounds like a Columbia
English major he's not gonna sell, so he puts on this other front.
Even just vocally he can produce that sound and make reason-
ably good music."

* * *

Some Crew members are ready to call it an evening, but others, especially Joyce and Paco, are still keen on debating the legitimacy of white participation in their culture. A typical Writers Crew session: from exposure to the revolutionary rhetoric of Fanon, to an exploration of the origins of street rap, to soul-searching about what this means to the Crew members as individuals, and now to a discussion of authentic rap culture and why some "white boys" have a true claim to share in it.

In the papers or on television tomorrow, editorials and cautionary tales will once again talk about the difficulty, if not impossibility, of racial understanding, or give one-sided portraits of desperate lives of teenagers in the so-called black underclass. But as the kids gather up their things and trade the warm gestures of a Harlem leave-taking, these dire pontifications seem off the mark. Indeed, they are a part of the Coca-Cola culture the kids are so fervent about rejecting.

In Terry Williams's suddenly empty apartment there is a letdown one can almost touch. If only the better, the more enduring part of life could be what goes on in the Writers Crew's discussions and readings, and the kids could be safe from the dangers and temptations of the street. If only . . . But that unavoidable parental impulse flies in the face of what makes them unique and strong and what it is they are creating in the Writers Crew.

Asking Blanche' how she liked the feeling. After a while Blanche' could only moan. Her thinking had been unclear and she couldn't get it together to say anything. Anthony finished undressing Blanche' LAID and laid her down on the carpet.

For the next few hours Blanche' and Anthony engaged in sex without his condoms sex and her diaphrams.

The next morning Blanche' woke up on the living room floor very hungry. She couldn't remember a thing from last night. She looked at the clock and realized she was over an hour late for work.

"Anthony" she called through the house while she held on to the couch to help support her when she stood up. "Anthony are you here?" She got no answer. Blanche' went into the bathroom and washed her face. She ran a cold shower and hopped in right quick and within a few minutes was out the door rushing off to work.

6

A page from Marisa's journal

Discipline and
Temptation

The effect of my sex will perplex
your mind, emotion, your temple.
Pleasure temple.
To find the secrets will be simple, ripple . . .
As I ride your . . . train, ride the rails so deep
I'll touch your brain.
Make you rain on my train, like an overcast.
Light your fuse,
count down.
It's time to blast off.

Paco's journal (1992)

After months of working together, the kids in the Writers Crew are more comfortable among themselves, even able to tease one another about things that concern them. Teasing is part of adolescence; it masks serious conduct and conflict. "Adolescence," it should be pointed out, is itself a misleading code word, for it suggests similarities in experience that cannot be assumed. There are too many paths along which young people are developing within the so-called adolescent years. Early adolescents are dealing with changes in their bodies, with forming close ties to peers, with learning how to behave in public, and this explains in large part why they are so frantic about conforming. To be told at age twelve that your sneakers are cheap or your clothes are poor is devastating to your self-image; when you are several years older, such comments may have little meaning to you.

For the kids uptown, where the trappings of conformity are harder to come by, such concerns as dress and appearance may take on great importance. But as the years pass, from early to later adolescence, even bigger, more intense challenges loom. These young people must face living in multiple worlds, the world of their own race, the world of the street, for instance, versus the white world, the world of school; they must face problems of independence and sexuality, of expressing needs and desires, and dealing with the consequences; they must face the search for places to develop their skills outside the family; and they must face growing pressures from inside the home they are preparing to leave and from outside it as well.

Living in Two Worlds:
Culture-Crossing

Dexter, back from looking into a downtown job prospect that didn't materialize, is talking with some other Crew members. He's thinking less about the unsuccessful job hunt than about his girlfriend, Velma. She's putting pressure on him to spend money on her, money he doesn't have. "She's been paying for everything lately because I don't have the duckets [money] like I used to. But you know, I believe girls—excuse me, women— are on a mission for equality in society, and in my own relationship I'm having a problem. My girl is on this equality trip too. I was listening to the radio and this guy was talking about heroes and sheroes, and this female came into the conversation and said, 'It's about time they mentioned women as hero-worshiping beings,' and all this stuff, and this made me mad. I think one of the biggest problems for black people is between females and males." Dexter is asked why women can't be seen as equal, since they are, and after considering for a moment, he says: "Yeah, but they want to take over the men. That's the problem. Once they get to that level they are trouble. First, they can fuck better and longer, especially longer, than men. They can reason just as good as men. They can build their muscles just like men. Just check out that gladiator show and shit. Them women look like men." He laughs. "So I say if you let 'em get in control, it's all over."

While females' perception of males moves in one direction—mainly about sex in exchange for their company—males feel it is pressure from females that creates more life-threatening situations. Dexter puts it squarely in the context of competition, another kind of market force. Girls demand rewards and favors that only money can buy. "I know that the boys risk their lives to be able to get with the females. All this scrambling [dealing] and shit is so we can get with them, because if you don't have that money you ain't nobody to them. They look at you and compare you with the kid on the block who's got crazy cash."

Some might not believe Dexter's explanation entirely, although there are powerful incentives to maintain the life-style once started; while many project boys risk their lives in the street, it is hardly done simply for sex or girls. On the other hand, the primary reason project boys deal drugs and take other physical and ethical risks is the money. The chance to be big-time on the block makes most dealers risk imprisonment and death. The perks include not only groupie girls and women, but the hustler's street fame, the power and prestige accorded only a few, and that fleetingly. Most women and girls in the neighborhood prefer men and boys with regular jobs over one drug dealer or another. As Jack says, "That would be a harsh blow to my ego if I couldn't get wid a girl with my rap and that the only way to get a girl would be to deal some drugs. That's some wack shit. You know, some guys want only these street girls, and they can't get these street girls with no nine-to-five. They can't get the girls that be with them dealers. Them girls can only be captured by flash and cash."

Sheena looks at female roles from a perspective that reflects her awareness of dangers for teenage girls and young adult women. "You might have skeezers [women who have sex for drugs and/or little or no money] out there, but they also be going back and forth to the clinics too [Health Department for testing for venereal disease]. Because they be having problems sleeping around with all them boys. But I think they are doing all the wrong things. They should be protecting our men and not putting pressure on them to deal drugs. When are we gonna get the girls to understand that they have to protect our men?"

The demands on kids in the projects and the city more generally border on the absurd—at least to adults outside this culture. The pressures on adolescent girls to have babies or boys to make illegal money are immense. It is generally assumed that teenage girls' ignorance about birth control is the reason many have children out of wedlock. But girls in the "baby crews," informal groups of adolescent girls who have babies for social and, sometimes, political reasons, challenge this idea. There are other opinions. "I think some of these girls have babies because of pressure," says Dexter, "but most of them ain't doing it because they want to increase the nation either. Maybe some of the boys are into that making-more-male-babies stuff but not as many of the girls are into that." Sheena sees entirely different reasons. "A lot of these girls have these babies to keep a man, plain and simple. Another reason they be getting pregnant is the best-friend thing: One of the girls will get pregnant by accident, and then her best friend will get pregnant too. The best friend didn't get pregnant because she didn't know no better, but so she could stay in with her circle of friends."

It is no secret motherhood is a world unto itself, from which women without babies are excluded. And many teenagers, wanting to be a part of that world, have babies in order to conform. They justify their behavior in various ways, as Marisa elaborates: "Some of the girls say they have babies to make the African nation in America strong, because black males are endangered. Some talk about having girls so that more girls gets more boys and children in general because the nation of black people is being destroyed by AIDS and death. But I think that's a minority of black teenage girls who are into that. Most of them are still very ignorant about how they get pregnant in the first place. Anyway you look at it, there is still a lot a pressure on black girls in these projects to rise above all of this." Whether the "baby crews" provide an identity or a means of gaining recognition or both—most crews do—they support individual talent and achievement and are increasingly a group of choice for adolescent girls.

For both sexes, the journey to reach maturity with self-esteem unblemished and the approval of their peers is arduous. Take, for example, the opposition Sheena encountered in one of her friends because she refused to use slang.

"I don't like to use slang words all that much, and my girlfriend told me I was acting white because I wasn't using slang. I looked at her like she had two heads instead of that one big one she's got. I said, 'Girl, you and the rest of your girls are cah-ray-zy, and y'all better get back some smarts if you want to make it out here.' "

Marisa recounts similar experiences. "Growing up in the projects is no picnic. There were people I didn't even know hating me just because I went to school and they thought it was cool to skip classes. I didn't skip none of my classes. My mother wouldn't let me go outside and be with everybody else, so people thought I was stuck-up. All I could do was just look out the window most of the time. But I went to school and this created problems for me. Most of the kids in the projects in a certain clique didn't go to school. They would hang out, they would go to the Cosmo [a local movie theater]. I went to school because I wanted to be somebody. And you know what? Those kids are now men and women, and many of them still sitting around the projects doing nothing."

Many kids have the notion that not conforming to street culture, acting "proper" or "white," means betraying one's friends, and indeed one's race. The pressure to conform is great, and the search for safe passage difficult. Adolescents, especially those with weak egos or little social support, are constantly struggling to reach their potential, and they face enormous demands to remain loyal to uptown culture if they attempt to cross cultures by going downtown. Dexter, for example, was badgered by drug-dealing friends to join their crew and not take a regular job. These boys, who used to be his "best friends in the 'hood," called him a "chump" and a "sissy" for not complying, and he was left with the choice of being forever taunted as a weakling or leaving the neighborhood. Sometimes, Dexter says, he doesn't know what to do, which path to follow. "I don't know how you do it," he tells Terry Williams. "How do you deal with them white boys downtown and then come back uptown and do research and live with the brother up here? When I go to school and I come back out here in the street, my boys say I'm wasting my time in school. I know it's best for me, but I gotta have my homeys because we been together for so long. But I gotta be different when I'm in school and around white folk. I gotta be different again when I come out here. I feel like I'm living in two worlds. I can't go into either one completely, and I can't get out of either one completely."

Six months later Dexter feels he can function well in both worlds, but he tends to "overindulge in the uptown trip, because I fall back into quick money. When I go uptown I see my mom struggling, and I see my need to survive. I need money no matter how it comes—legal, illegal. I get frustrated because I'm tired of living where I'm living. It gets depressing. People be smoking in my building. They be pitching [dealing] in there too."

When he gets off the subway from downtown and sees his friends, Dexter says, they "hang and drink beer or whatever." Yet "the pressure is there no matter what I'm doing—maybe not all the time verbally, but it's there. Most of this pressure uptown is negative. But I can swing downtown and do the telephone-survey stuff. I can tell graduate students to do this and do that, and I swing uptown and tell my people to do this and do that. Sometimes I hit a pothole and lose control. That's a problem: I lose control."

Jack has his own experiences in culture-crossing. "I was always around white folk because my uncle, who is a famous musician, was always introducing white folk to me. I went to school with white kids, and I have had jobs in places where it really ain't no big deal. My homeboys understand this, and I can go downtown with my tie and suit and do what I have to do there."

As the kids venture outside of the Harlem environment, they gain experience in how to conduct themselves in other social settings. Terry Williams is an important role model in this respect, along with other adults with whom he puts the kids in contact. He seeks to influence them subtly, indirectly, seldom telling them what to do or how to act; rather, by his very presence and in small daily interactions, he projects possibilities of comportment that sometimes mirror, sometimes challenge their customary ways of acting. Once, for example, Terry took Dexter, Sheena, and Marisa to the Russell Sage Foundation, where he was working. Dexter had on a slick leather cap, which he wore jauntily to the side. On the street, and among his peers, the cap had a certain meaning; in the professional environment of Russell Sage, it did not have the same resonance. Terry nudged him and told him to remove the cap. A bit surprised, Dexter did so. Later, in Terry's house, Dexter asked if he should take off the cap. Terry told him he could do as he liked. Terry was trying to communicate to Dexter that while his wearing the cap was a form of cultural and personal expression that should be valued, he should at the same time be sensitive to milieu, to cultural codes beyond his own; Dexter and the others should not deny their own roots or embrace another cultural code exclusively, yet they needed to develop sensitivity in order to expand his room for operation.

By showing them "appropriate" behavior, and by discussing and introducing them to unaccustomed worlds, Terry hopes that the kids' perceptions and understandings of life will be expanded and enriched. In this way their possibilities are likewise expanded, and their critical reflection deepened.

Meanwhile, uptown kids face everyday realities in their own world, the projects. There is risk and trauma there, and such concerns as life, death, money, and sex play a constant refrain in the minds of project teenagers. Dexter, for instance, has flirted with fate and now realizes that death is an end, not a beginning. Sex is another story; it's the way he tries to find his happiness within the limits of project life. But even sex has its life-or-death clause. "At one time I risked my life for pussy," he says. "And many of my friends out here still do." Dexter recounts that he and other youths would do whatever they had to do to gain the attention and respect, and thus the company, of girls.

"In order for us to get respect, we got to put a posse together and go out and do what they do. Make some money. Once this happens, watch the ho's flock to us. So we go out and risk getting killed so we could be with them girls. So unless you ready to give up the sex or give up the drugs, give up the gun, you take the risk." Dexter's own posse did not last because the members disagreed on how the proceeds would be spent. He wanted to give some of their profit to the community by establishing a youth center with job skills training. The others wanted to keep the money and split it evenly among themselves. Dexter admits that there are various types of young women. "There are more girls besides these gangster bitches, who you gotta please with blood and money. What about the nice girls who you don't have to do that shit for."

Paco pulls a sheet of spotty, wrinkled yellow paper from his pocket, glances at it, then puts it back into his pocket. "Listen up, let me tell y'all my rap. It's called 'The Effect of My Sex': 'I want your sex. The effect of my sex will perplex your mind, emotion, your temple. Pleasure temple. To find the secrets will be simple, ripple. . . . As I ride your . . . train, ride the rails so deep I'll touch your brain. Make you rain on my train, like an overcast. Light your fuse, count down. It's time to blast off. Because the universe is calling. Ride a star, feel my planet. . . . With our sweat our bodies glide.' No, wait a minute—it's 'our bodies collide.' "

"What the fuck is it, man? 'Collide,' or 'glide,' or what?" someone asks. The Crew members laugh.

"Who wrote this drippy shit?" Dexter wonders.

Paco takes the sheet of paper out of his pocket again. But by now some of the other kids look uncomfortable. The talk now turns to the subjects of rape, race, and Mike Tyson.

Dexter and his friends say they are "risking their life for pussy"; Joyce and Tina have problems with this, and don't believe a word of it. Around women the boys rarely use the word "bitch" (for "woman"), except in abbreviated ways or in quotation marks; they say it is not a bad word but it has become politically incorrect. "Skeezer," on the other hand, is a bad word, for what in any small town in middle America might be called the town whore.

"What was Desiree Washington?" Dexter asks with a show of innocence. "Wasn't she a skeezer? Wasn't she just another ho' looking to get paid by a motherfucker who is known to risk his life for pussy?"

Joyce challenges Dexter's insinuations. She has been writing about the Tyson affair, and she reads from her piece: " 'Visions of skeezers danced in our heads. They haunted us as we tried to reconstruct the rationale of a woman who could wander into the bedroom of a man who spends his life waxing ass and disrespecting his dick—without expecting to give up the punanny. As creatures of the nightlife, we'd seen too many groupies riding the snoopies of the largest rapper/reverend/athlete/dealer in search of the vicarious power so many of us associate with status and dollars. It was hard to maneuver our feminist consciousness around the protective anonymity that surround an alleged rape victim. She was Lady X, and he was, in all his lecherous notoriety, Mike Tyson. Suspicious neutrality was the best we could muster.' "

"Mike Tyson don't be risking his life for pussy," Jack says, "he be risking his life for money. I'm tired of hearing the brothers say, 'It's the bitches' fault,' because American white folk with their racism and sexism and drugs and crime has made the brothers turn on each other. We become the walking wounded, the locked-up wounded, the ghettoized wounded, that disproportionately represent what's going on in America." These comments don't ring true coming from Jack, who often seems to have the most misogynistic attitude around. "Listen up, y'all. Let me kick this." He takes his dog-eared journal and starts to read about a scene his neighborhood: " 'This can be really disgusting sometimes, sitting here at about one o'clock in the morning during the summer, because that's when all the skeezers come out, all shapes and sizes. The term 'skeezer' is used for female crackheads who will do anything to get a jumbo [large bottle of crack]. Man, I have heard all kinds of skeezer stories, and sometimes they be funny and sometimes they're sad, because a lot of these sisters who are referred to as skeezers were at one time very beautiful black women from all types of backgrounds. I have had quite a few run-ins with different women of this nature, and most of them are very aware of the effects that can occur with this consistent indulgence of crack.' "

Tina points out that the black women caught in this mess are there as both blacks and women.

Joyce assumes a look of concern and power over the situation. "The men who define black women's struggle encourage our complicity by convincing us that issues of race must precede those of gender. They have engaged us in a silent, cruel war that dictates its victims not speak of their persecution, so that we can remain one Afrocentric nation under a groove. But some of us don't buy the illusion. Our inability to swim the stormy sea between blackness and our womanness, our race loyalty and our humanity, forces us to ask the disturbing questions that black womanist author Pearl Cleage so bravely asked when she took Miles Davis's sexist brutality to task: How can they, she said, rape us and still be our heroes? How can they hit us and still be our leaders? Our husbands? Our lovers? Our geniuses? Our friends? And the answer is . . . they can't. Can they?"

Joyce goes on to talk about the way rap artists have reduced black women to "bitches" and "ho's." "Street brothers buy into that shit all the time by the way they treat us in the street." She is against the idea that black women have to suppress their feelings of ambiguity on the matter.

"Well, to be honest," Jack says, "I'm a little worried about my brothers too, Joyce." He utters this with complete sincerity. Those who know him fold their arms and look toward the ceiling. "I was sitting with my homeys in the park the other night and we somehow got into this discussion about the relationship between men and women. Everyone gave their opinion and I had come to the conclusion that women have men on a 'hype.' Some men are so confused because of how certain women respond or react to a lot of things that they just start flipping. Women are very unpredictable, and one of nature's most complex mysteries. That's why I'm so crazy about women. There is a lot we men could learn from women about our manhood, if we could get off that bus to Ego City."

"Get the fuck outta here, Jack," Dexter says. "We trying to have a serious conversation and you talking shit."

"No," Jack insists, "I am serious. Let me finish, my brother. It's really sad how women are exploited by men in this society. A lot of men don't understand women and what they are capable of accomplishing, and so the men get intimidated. Women do have that effect, and I think it's beautiful."

Joyce takes him to task. "You know, you are so full of it. Everybody knows you are the most blatant womanizer around.

You can't see a woman walking without saying something to her. I know your shit. I have witnesses."

As everyone else laughs and amens, Jack seems only amused by her comments.

Thoughts

The session continues with Tina's reading an open letter from her journal entitled "Thoughts." The letter offers some reflections on what she calls "bad vibes from men," and describes what many women experience on a daily basis: harassment by men on the street, male comments about their bodies, unwanted cooing at the women's every move, grabbing and touching without provocation—in other words, sexism often taken for granted in everyday life. When she was younger, Tina was raped by a boy who lived next door; she has suffered much pain and depression, and she still harbors angst toward men. She shares this story with the Writers Crew because she has heard others reveal their deepest feelings at meetings.

Tina has rarely shown up for Crew sessions. She came today, she says, because "this whole mess of feelings has welled up inside me and I want to talk about it." She agonized about the open letter and wasn't at all sure if the other Crew members would understand. "I don't want to reexamine my life in front of everybody," she tells the Crew. "I just want to read this because, you know, I have never even talked about all of this with my own mother. I told her certain parts, but not the whole affair. This letter doesn't quite tell everything, but it is more than I have told her. You should see it as basically a conversation I'm having with you."

I was repeatedly raped by "the boy next door" my freshman year of high school. That was eight years ago. Male violence against women is as American as apple pie. Television and movie screens reek of sexual violence. Women in print are used to satisfy male consumerism. Rap music has given birth to all sorts of bitches and ho's. Yet I dig Ice Cube. Kool G. Rap. L.L. Cool J. Brand Nubian. Lord Finesse. Slick Rick. I am a victim of this society's sexist jokes and those who follow through with violent crimes against women.

ONE

The D's, Dad and divorce, lead me searching for a piece of dad from boys and men who are basically dicks. But then there are the uncles. All of Papa's ace boon coons love and look out since there is no dad in New York City. I make Papa by taking a little piece of everyone and making them into one collective dad. Smile. It is now time to get to know my Main Man since his ever present love vanished after the divorce making me terribly insecure and very angry with him today. Peace.

TWO

I was terribly eager to have a boyfriend.

THREE

The schmuck lived on my floor in the building where I grew up. It's a very simple story. There's no need for any graphic details. I am simply sharing because at thirteen I would not have felt as alone if I knew how often women are raped in America. He knew and now my mother hates him. Like smoking cigarettes and experimenting with herb and alcohol it was an act of rebellion. Girls with good sense knew he was trash. Any girl with good sense would not spend her time with her "boyfriend" who was a pothead and addicted to cocaine smooching in the hallways of her building. I was insecure and therefore attracted to him. It's difficult to admit, however, it's the truth. He'd always appear in the hallway after hearing our door close or when I was leaving a girlfriend's apartment. Heavy petting in the hallway continued through the summer. The week before ninth grade I went shopping. In his bright orange tee-shirt, jeans and Adidas, he saw me from his window, waited by the elevator on our floor, dragged me to his apartment and attempted to rape me. I began closing my door quietly and using the building's staircases rather than riding the elevator. My method was not successful the night before my fourteenth birthday. He claimed he would tell my mother if I did not submit to his sexual needs. I believed him. The summer after the school year my soul was cleansed by spending three months with my father in Africa. When I returned to New York City, I stopped speaking to him. The second day of tenth grade he stooped to dragging me down the hallway as a retarded neighbor spotted him.

FOUR

On my seventeenth birthday, I told my mother about the rape. Mother let me know there is no way she could be angry with me which I found very supportive and loving. It's affected me negatively for every year I let pass and without dealing with the fact that a violent crime was committed against me and I don't want the normality of rape to continue.

FIVE

I was so lacking in confidence that no boys liked me in high school. One of my classmates was killed by a Mack truck in the South Bronx during the spring junior year. I expressed my anger by getting to the point where I was sick at any Dalton party. At the end of the school year one of Dalton's finest boys asked me to the prom. It spread around school that afternoon like no other piece of gossip since he's white and I'm black. I got sick at the prom. Senior year of high school I knew I had to go to an all-women's college since I'd been stripped of my self-confidence between the divorce, Dalton and rape.

SIX

I spent first semester with my father and joined all my women's feminist academic institution in the boonies of Pennsylvania for the next year and a half. I left being disgusted with the realization that I was at an Ivory tower. I could not deal with a library that only catered to everything that is western and European White! I got sick of white women's version of feminism and the concept of being "politically correct."

SEVEN

New York. Cotton-Lycra. And why is it that we (women) dress half naked? Cotton lycra cannot be worn by a woman above Fourteenth Street otherwise she will be sexually harassed in the streets. The day I wore cotton lycra on the train, men undressed me with their eyes. I'm wearing jeans and a Mickey Mouse tee-shirt when some man asks where the number 6 train is. I don't know. He glares at me and says, "Come here, woman!" I say, *"Fuck you!"* This behavior is not limited to the streets. I'm the only female in an office filled with men. Someone plays a song by Eazy-E of N.W.A. telling some girl how to suck his dick. Someone asked if I learned anything. The Jungle Brothers' performance of their song "Black Woman" appears quite phony. Last week, I got into this intense argument with a guy I like. I'm totally turned on by making him angry to the point where we're grabbing and pulling on each other in between words. Maleness, macho-ness, and violence that's equated with love is totally unhealthy yet I enjoy it.

I am sharing my thoughts with you at the tail end of adolescence. I'm sure you, like me, have been brainwashed by sexism and may not always confront and question the ways women are dominated by men in American Society. I will stop searching for my dad and actually get to know my father. Mainly, I'm sharing as a person concerned with sexism and particularly that which leads to violence against women. Peace.

Tina finishes reading and looks as if a heavy load has been lifted from her. After a silence, Sheena finally says, "That was one of the best pieces I've heard anybody read from their journal. That was so good it made me wanna cry." There is a chorus of approval for Tina, and in a few minutes the talk turns once again to sex and language, hip-hop and rap.

Sexual Flavors

Teenagers are less repressed than adults when it comes to matters of sex, and African-American and Latino inner-city youth are particularly free about expressing their sexuality. Their music, dance, dress, language, movement, and daily activities attest to their freedom in expression. Hip-hop shouts its explicit lyrics, dance videos explode in gyrating sensuality, and comedy routines are equally forthright. Rap music is one of the most direct media for teenagers to voice their sexuality; and consequently it has met more and more frequently with opposition ranging from conservative editorials to overt censorship. This conservative reaction, religious and otherwise, comes from white as well as black individuals and institutions. Indeed, the Reverend Calvin Butts, minister one of the largest black churches in New York City, recently spoke out against rap artists who rely on provocative lyrics and videos.

This openness about sexuality, then, is conveyed linguistically as well as physically, and nowhere is that more clearly demonstrated than in the projects and the streets of New York. The young people's sexual language is, as might be expected, energetic, and provocative; it aims to stimulate. Malika, Keisha, and Shaniqua, teenage friends of Dexter's who are interested in the Writers Crew, describe a "boody call," in which a young man or woman phones someone after midnight in an attempt to have sex.

"We all got the party line going," Malika says. "One of us will call another one and then get a hookup. Keisha calls and says she wants some dick, and that triggers the sexual flavors.

Shaniqua wants to call her boyfriend, she's in need of S-E-X. Right?"

Shaniqua agrees: "I'm in bed and shit."

"Yeah," Keisha says, "but you should be fucking, because Leroy's got it going on."

"You know he wants the pussy," Malika tells Shaniqua.

"I wanna beep him, then. It is past midnight."

"Damn, girl, you gotta beep for dick?" Keisha asks.

"Fuck you, bitch, it's better than waiting for somebody to call. You gotta get up on it," Shaniqua responds, and then announces, "Hold on, I'm gonna beep him. Ooh, I know, why don't you beep him for me, Malika, and put in my number so I won't tie up the line."

Malika beeps for Shaniqua. "Are you satisfied?" she asks.

"No. I won't be satisfied until I get some balls in my mouth."

"Oh bitch, you don't even know how to suck dick," Keisha taunts.

"Oh yes I do," Shaniqua insists. "He taught me."

"Oh yeah? I bet he didn't teach you how to hum on balls."

"Hum on balls?"

"Let's put her down on it," Malika says to Keisha. "We know the bitch uses her teeth too much." There is laughter all around, as a call comes in from the beeper.

"That's the boody call," Malika and Keisha say giggling. "Get one in for us, girl."

———

Wanting Sex and
Getting Sex

Sheena shows up an hour early for a weekly Crew meeting; she has plenty on her mind, especially her daughter, her grandmother, and men. When the session starts she reads passages about her early sex life from her journal. Sex came early for her, and she thought the experience was positive, until she became addicted to it. She did not want to be branded or stereotyped. " 'A great lover I may call myself, not a slut, but someone who is well experienced at a young age.' " By the age of fourteen she was " 'at the point of losing my mind and my virginity all at once. I would shift in all directions, try to encounter new things. Sex was a major role, drugs was the input, for my damaged computer brain, but not too bad when it came to drugs. No LSD, no needles, no pills, but beer and liquor and pot. Something that would always make my eyes red and my brain dead and it would make me cough. I hated that. Yes, I was rather fast.' "

Sheena says it is hard to explain her complex story. She reads on: " 'I would like to express how I went from a child to a woman in a decade. Yes . . . it took me ten years to figure out what my life was all about, and it still has me bewildered. Sometimes I say, How odd and very complicated I make my life out to be each day. I've had many ups and downs. I have come across some rainbows that were blown away. I've hit some blizzards that have lasted more than they should have. I've been to the gates of hell a couple of times, but my dear friend Michael [her boyfriend] always seems to help me survive. I think I was put here for a great purpose. Maybe it will come to me one day.' "

After her mother died, Sheena lost faith in "all matters of reality"; significantly, she began failing at school. But like most adolescents, she had dreams of doing better; hope was still a part of her life. "My family thought it was just a phase I was going through. They knew I was smart and all I needed was time to get myself together." Yet Sheena wanted to explore more than the life around home and school and sought to "mingle with the real world."

Around this time her steady boyfriend did not force her to have sex but did manipulate her in other ways. "He was very successful in dominating me," she says. "He did this for almost the entire four years of our relationship. He wanted me to cut my hair, so I did. I can't blame the boy for anything. I made my own mistake. As far as school was concerned, he did not want to date a dummy. He wanted the best for me in that category. He pressured me into staying in my classes, but I would not listen."

Her boyfriend insisted she stop smoking, then demanded her to have sex with him on a regular basis and show that she enjoyed it. "I didn't enjoy the experience at first. He couldn't make me like it. It wasn't the best, or the worst, but it took us four months to get it right, at least for me to enjoy it. After that it was sensational and I became a little nymphomaniac."

Within a year she was pregnant and had had her first abortion. By age fifteen she was engaging in sex with boys besides her boyfriend; by age sixteen she was having sex four days a week. In high school, she says, she made all her mistakes. She cut classes regularly and engaged in street fights; she acted out her hostility with everyone. "I was so vain, so full of hatred. I was smart, but very dumb. I spent more time in the dean's office than the dean did."

Actually, the dean of the school was fond of Sheena and thought she had potential, but felt she carried around too much emotion, too much angst. The dean, Sheena says, "did love me and always tried to get me out of trouble. And now that I think about it, she was right: I was too emotional. When I came to her office crying, she knew it was because a teacher had upset me. I thought I couldn't handle school anymore."

Sheena did find a few things she could handle at school, however: "Every day I was in school I made it my business to hang around the security guards. I always liked to flirt. I had many associates. Everybody knew me. I was said to be very attractive and had beautiful skin, and nice legs. Boys always loved my legs. I had no ass, mind you. Yeah, that was my complex. I was never really shaped the way I dreamed I could be. Always pretty teeth, pretty smile, big breasts, slender legs, nice hair, soft skin—but no ass. It just didn't fit. But men always fell in love with me anyway. I never had a problem getting a man to like me. I was the charmer."

Yet she was unhappy and started drinking, mostly by herself, and crying at the slightest provocation. She would walk alone in Central Park, where the breeze and the sounds of crisp leaves beneath her feet seemed to relax her. Sometimes she would walk from her high school on 84th Street to 42nd Street, where she would play games in a video arcade. "There were many kids like me, but I never really bothered to be with them. I decided if I was to get in trouble in school, it would always be best to be by myself. That is why I got off the hook so many times. Maybe teachers felt sorry for me. I understood my work, but never did it."

On one day when she did not attend school, Sheena headed to Macy's with fifty dollars of her grandmother's money. Before entering the store she was sidetracked by a three-card monte game on the street. "I saw people playing with these cards and it looked easy. In my bra was twenty-five dollars, in my hand was fifty. I gambled all fifty dollars, and before I knew it I had lost it. I went home crying." Then, to make matters worse, she went to a police station and said she had been robbed, and later repeated the story to her grandmother. "I told her that terrible lie. I was afraid to tell the truth. My grandmother had a good idea that I was lying. I finally told her the truth."

But Sheena continued lying to her grandmother about other things. On one occasion she claimed that she had been assaulted. She and her boyfriend had been out for a long time, and Sheena knew she should go home. She did not return until after eleven, at least two hours late. "I ripped my blouse and messed up my hair and said someone tried to rape me. That was really cold. My grandmother went outside with a ice pick, looking for the man I described. I finally told her the truth."

All of these situations began to take their toll on Sheena's family. "Everyone in my family thought I was losing all of my screws," Sheena says. While her family believed she needed help, she understood one fundamental problem: "being afraid to tell the truth."

At sixteen Sheena was considering suicide. She felt her

friends were not interested in her for herself; they always wanted something from her. She dated a teen drug dealer for a while, ignoring the obvious signs of his profession. "I dated a boy who would not work, although when I met him he was working. He seemed to be so hyper all the time, and he lied about everything. I come to find out he was on drugs. He sniffed cocaine. The only way he would get turned on is if I told him filthy stories, which I was good at because of my wild imagination. I was never into sex games too hot. No bondage or threesomes. I thought they were rather disgusting. I dated him for a long time and he eventually helped me run away from home."

After a year with this young man, Sheena went back home. She had dropped out of school, and now she was pressured by her family to return and finish. "I wanted to correct my mistakes, but I was lost. I did not know where to begin. I was in so much trouble, and my family hated me. They assumed I was becoming my mother all over again."

Sheena's grandmother tried to be patient with her, but she was hurt too. She felt Sheena had let her down. She tried, out of frustration, to take her to court, but could not go through with it. "I think she was just trying to scare me," Sheena says. "I was her baby from two on up." Sheena's brother had begun to act out as well. He "started to rebel. I guess he figured if I could do it, so could he. He's five years younger than I am and I love him to death, but I didn't want him to be worse than I was." Instead of abandoning hope, Sheena turned to a psychiatrist for help. By her own assessment the doctor "did some good for a short while." Her family too offered her and her brother support. "My uncle bought games for my brother and a big stereo for me. My grandmother got extra money from him each month and an air conditioner. My grandmother gave us cable. So actually, my brother and I had no reason to rebel. Why did we? I can tell you all I wanted to do was be grown, too soon. I wasn't ready for the real world, but still I wanted to be free. I thought, If I make mistakes, I'll correct them myself.

"I do love my grandmother very much, but I had my opinion and she and the rest of my family had theirs. You would not believe how this woman has stuck by my side. She would yell at me, then when I got ready to go out ask me if I need money. She thinks she's a fool for all this love. She thinks she's getting no feedback, and when I look at it she isn't, and I am very sorry for troubling her all these years the way I have. Sometimes parents can be so right that it makes you want to rebel. My grandmother would say, 'Don't stay out late,' only because it was dangerous, and I would stay out anyway. I would always come up with some bullshit. I was good at that. I felt nobody could tell me what to do."

Sheena was six months pregnant and on her way to see her grandmother when she and the baby's father decided to leave the cab without paying the fare. She fell and broke her ankle and was hospitalized. She thought she might lose the baby. "I was almost unconscious. I had a broken ankle, cuts and bruises. When police asked the cabbie what had happened, he said we robbed him. I didn't know this at the time. Around midnight my boyfriend was arrested."

Three months later, with her baby's father gone and only her grandmother to care for her, Sheena developed a new appreciation for life when her baby was born. "I had been through hell. There was no one in my corner but my sweet grandmother. How could she love someone like me, who did not appreciate anything she had done for me while I was growing up? I can't help feeling guilty. I do pray for her. God knows how sorry I am for all the mistakes I have made. My grandmother tells me she loves me dearly and I know that. My brother and I mean the world to her. I want her to realize I know I made mistakes, but I was beginning to think they weren't mistakes anymore. I was following the same steps as my mother. My baby's father wanted me to have an abortion, but I wanted my child. I wanted to have my baby more than ever. I know I have no money but welfare will do for a while. I know I can't stay on it forever."

Sheena's grandmother made space for the baby in her own room and bought clothing for Sheena and the baby. No one else offered to help. "Of course, my family thought this was the last straw, to have a baby at seventeen. They couldn't even stand to look at me. My friends wanted to give me a shower, but now my baby was already here."

Sheena, like many teenage girls, had to face the reality that her life was changing permanently. She could no longer engage in the free-spirit living she was accustomed to before Xiamara's birth. She found herself on another side of adolescent life, no boyfriend, no job, a mother and alone.

Dexter

In the Washington projects on the east side of Harlem, Dexter sits in his room thinking about his future. His mother has been trying to make him leave home to find a job. When he did find one, he didn't stay employed long enough to save money for an apartment. This added strain to already difficult circumstances at home.

Dexter started working in a drug-dealing crew at age fifteen. "All the old-timers, kids twenty, twenty-one, twenty-two, made money in the business," he says. "I just wanted to get paid too. High school was not happening, really. My high school was one big fashion statement. I didn't have the cash to keep coming up dapper and fresh every day, back to back to back." He was ready to learn from the street but resolved never to be defeated by its harshness. He vowed also never to be hungry; he wanted to make his mother proud of him. He brought money home but did not tell her what he was doing—only that he was working part-time to help out. His mother expected this help to continue even after he was arrested with other neighborhood boys for running their drug business. Her subtle hints for him to make money or leave home were a way of saying he could sell drugs or do anything else as long as he brought money. Mrs. Wells never stated in so many words that she didn't care what Dexter did, but her actions toward him, and her callous disregard for his successful attempts to make something of himself clearly indicate a dislike for the boy. Dexter often mentions her indifference to his accomplishments.

A producer from National Public Radio asked Dexter if he would like to write commentary for a program; he would be paid modestly for three minutes of his musings on teenage life in the projects. Dexter accepted the offer and happily rushed home to tell his mother. She was interested only in how much he would be paid. This was neither the first time nor the last that she would ignore his achievements and focus on what Dexter considers the most crass aspect of things. On another occasion, Dexter was appearing in television interviews and conducting them for a study arranged by Bill Kornblum—all part of a project to learn social science skills and develop analytical thinking. This education was apparently of little concern to Mrs. Wells. She asked Terry Williams how much her son was getting paid, then criticized Dexter's efforts and said he should be getting more money. It is not that Dexter doesn't value money—quite the contrary: he constantly asks whether he will be paid for this task or that media interview, and often doesn't understand why some media entities pay for interviews and some don't.

"My mother don't care about what happens to me one way or the other," Dexter says, and he complains that he is never complimented for doing good. For her part, Mrs. Wells says that she doesn't want him doing anything wrong. "If he's not making any money doing all of what he's doing, then why do it? He knows I need help around here and he has to pay his way." While Mrs. Wells says she doesn't want her son doing anything wrong, he says she never asked where the money was coming from when he was part of the drug crew. When they talked, it was always at her initiative, and she mistrusts him. "She be always trying to catch me in a lie."

Dexter describes how he started to resent his mother and not care what she had to say. He felt she should provide for him because he was her son. She began to resent his eating and sleeping all day and not working when the part-time jobs ended, and tried to force him out. Dexter resisted the pressure to leave: if she could play games, so could he.

What Dexter sees but perhaps has chosen to ignore is how poor his family is. His mother cannot afford to pay bills and keep food on the table. He is unmoved by all of this. If he had to suffer, he thinks, so would she. He would be as defiant and uncommunicative as possible to wreak the maximum psychological havoc. When he got money he would give her only a scant amount, and only after she asked for it a few times.

Last year Dexter met his father for the first time. "I had only talked to him for twenty minutes, when I was nine years old. So when I see him he ain't got nothing to say to me. He just sit there and ask how I'm doing, and I say I'm fine, and that was about it. He got another family, with a bunch of girls and one boy who looks like me. But it ain't no mystery no more now. It's over. But I had to go find him after my brother calls. He never came here looking to find out what happened to me. But check my little brother out. His pops, my moms, and me. See. They be poppin' shit behind my back, and I know it, I know it. They got their little family, and then there's me. I don't have my own room. I don't have my own phone. I don't have nothing but me."

Dexter lives in two worlds. He is drawn to the street and his neighborhood, yet recognizes the pressure to get ahead in the white world downtown. He is ambivalent about what his black friends will say about his "acting white" and at the same time conflicted about that behavior and the culture it represents.

"I should be controlling this block, man," Dexter mumbles as he surveys his street. He seems to be daydreaming about taking over the drug trade in his neighborhood. He knows he

will never engage in that kind of illegality again, but he fanta-
sizes nevertheless. "I should not have to be chumped off every
time one of my friends comes by in a new BMW and I ain't got
a dollar in my fucking pocket. Them Puerto Rican motherfuckers are out here, but hey, they just punks, man, they just punks.
We could take 'em. My posse and me could have this block
tomorrow. Sometimes I could just mow 'em down. I came out
here one day and I just had this look to kill in my eyes. If I had
art [artillery] that day I woulda hurt somebody. I should be
gettin' paid out here."

"Gettin' paid," reaping the benefits of not only the drug
trade but any and all illegal activity, entails organizing a crew
with a vertical structure in which he would be the boss. While
other crew members would do the actual selling, Dexter would
supply the contraband and stake out and maintain his territory,
one block at a time. The block he lives on is uncontrolled for
now, that is, no one group has absolute authority and all comers
can compete for customers. On a controlled block, one crew
alone sells drugs and it allows no other sellers in the area.

Unemployment is high in Dexter's neighborhood, as it is all
over Harlem. About sixty percent of the teenagers in the community are looking for legal work. Changes over the last ten to
twenty years in the New York City economy, especially the shift
from manufacturing to service employment, have reduced
young African-Americans and Latinos to alienated "potential
workers." Many members of minority groups made their place in
the city at manufacturing jobs, which abounded in the fifties,
sixties, and seventies. Young adults from the projects, Dexter
among them, have no such chance today, as those jobs have
dried up.

Dexter recognizes this lack, and sees a futility in job training. "There ain't no jobs," he says. "What do I need training for
when there ain't no jobs to go to?" Dexter's mother has provided
little guidance; indeed, she has given contradictory signals to
him about participating in the drug trade. Like many poor par-

ents, in not discouraging him from underground activity, she effectively gives him an esteem-building nod to continue.

Most project families believe in hard work and education, but many youths see low-level jobs as demeaning, alienating, and culturally exploitative. Creating jobs for teenagers in or near the projects is a problem. An agency in charge of summer jobs for youth sees, on the average, 5,000 teens seeking 200 jobs. Cyril James, a counselor at a youth employment agency, says many teens turn to selling drugs when they do not find other work in the neighborhood. Even if they find summer work, he says, "these kids know they need work all year round. They supplement that summer work by selling drugs in the fall."

Dexter, who has worked legally—as an errand boy, a dishwasher, and a supermarket bagger—aspires to be respected for more than the qualities the next hustler brings to the street. He has been through enough trauma to consider his options. He didn't have the luxury of a father, his mother resents him, he has seen friends die, he has dropped out of school. He has walked around at times with only pennies in his pocket. He wants the guidance of internal controls—his own motivation, intelligence, and positive values—not external controls such as the parole board and threats of more jail time. Although he occasionally contemplates getting back into the drug business, he knows these thoughts are only a mind game. The likelihood of his being punished for committing an illegal act is much greater now than before because he is on probation, and he is not about to take the risk. There was a time when he didn't care about the consequences of his actions, but that was when he was a kid.

Dexter has, however, violated parole and is supposed to see his probation officer. He says his fate is being "played" by strangers, who are part of an impersonal criminal injustice system. He suggests that Terry Williams meet with his probation officer. "She's West Indian and hard on me, real hard. If you could talk to her and chill her out and see what the problem is, I would feel a lot better. She told me I should have told her I was leaving the country, and I would have gotten permission. But I didn't wanna take the chance."

The story is more involved than that. Dexter wanted to go on a trip with his girlfriend to Barbados. According to the conditions of his probation, which runs for five years, he is not to leave the borough of Manhattan without permission from his probation officer. He claims she would not have allowed him to go if he had asked. Around the same time he added another violation to his record, when he was arrested for jumping a subway turnstile.

When Terry meets with Dexter's probation officer, he emphasizes his potential as a good citizen and mentions his participation in the Writers Crew. While she is reluctant, the probation officer says she is willing to forgive Dexter this time. If he did not violate parole again, his probation might be over sooner than expected.

Dexter and older teenagers in the projects all talk about pressure. It's a developmental feature, and ever present for most of them. When they reach their late teens, girls and especially boys are "pushed out" of the family. Poor parents look at the cost of the food their children eat, the price of the clothes they wear, and consider their age and behavior; their children are adults, they feel, and by age eighteen should take care of themselves, or at least help the family.

Many boys who consider themselves "street" have tried dealing drugs; girls are minor players in the trade. There is pressure on males to act and look a certain way in order to impress females. The latter compete for boys by providing sexual favors or, if they are "good girls," go to school and "do the right thing" by parents and other concerned adults whom they respect.

Many kids who start off seeking "sneaker money" in the

drug trade, when they see they are "doing all right," choose to continue "until something happens," says Jack. These kids have a burning need for money: "You need money in your pocket to go to movies, buy sneakers, buy pizzas, things like that. It's basically, you know, Mo' money, mo' money."

Sheena adds that they may "feel more independent than working part-time in a supermarket or something like that. All they have to do is sit out there on the bench and sell these drugs. You go outside and sit on a bench anyway."

Dexter describes some of his friends who have dealt drugs: "They would rather be their own boss. You gotta understand that not all of them be hustling. At least a handful of them work, but sometimes not for long. They may work in supermarkets and the fast-food places for a minute. They do that and sell drugs too. As a matter of fact, they work in these places in order to make enough money to save up to buy material to deal. And when the drug business starts to boom they leave the legit job and go dealing full-time. That part's not understood, because with the drugs they can make so much money. Even when they don't make big money, they keep trying to make it. They be making something. You see, the drugs are always there and anybody can get into it. And everybody want to be wid it"—popular and successful. Although some kids may not want to deal, for various reasons, including the fear of being caught, Dexter continues, "they do it anyway. They just do it out of envy or jealousy, not because they hungry. If you're doing it because you see your friend doing it and you see all the stuff he got and you want to get it, that's the wrong reason. Jealousy or envy is not the reason you want to be out here dealing these drugs. You gotta do it because you're hungry.

"Everybody be making small money anyway," Dexter insists. "The reason you don't see so many people making big money is because they are so many small-time hustlers doing it, and they be pushed together—it's like everybody is all over everybody else. It's like on every other block. So whoever is smoking it have so many different people to cop from. Let's say he go here to the corner and they selling for five dollars and they two dollar short, well, they can just go to the other corner where they selling for three dollars. And that's where the conflicts come in, with the pistols and the fighting."

Dexter talks about the use or threatened use of nine-milli-meter weapons as a way to counter violence. "A few years ago we were standing on the corner spot where my posse and me work, and these other kids came by to take over the spot. We just stood our ground and flash them nines, and they stepped off. We used to make six, seven hundred [dollars] a day in that spot, and in no way were we gonna let them chumps take over."

Drug dealing is based on a consignment method: drugs are given to street dealers with no payment up-front but with the understanding that they will pay their suppliers back once they have sold their merchandise. If this trust is broken, by vendors who receive drugs but don't pay up later, violence is often the result. Drug dealing in the projects means close physical con-nections between buyers and sellers, and between sellers and suppliers. It is difficult to hide. Jack, who doesn't live in the projects but who hangs out there with some of his homeboys, talks about trust and violence. "You can't be dealing out here without the trust thang. And you know that. You get a cap busted in yo' ass if you frontin' on somebody with they cash or they dope. If them kids think you holding out on them, they get you. They get you good. Them niggers be cold crazy out here."

A male teenager's street reputation is of utmost importance: Is he seen by peers as "soft," weak or unmanly, or as having "heart"? Does he command respect, or is he easily "dissed"? A male teenager's reputation, indeed his very life, often depends on apparently minor gestures or behavior: looking at another boy's girlfriend, stepping on someone's foot, winning in a con-test of ritual insult, or in the case of dealing, letting a debtor talk openly about not paying his debt. These are all considered "uncivil" acts in a city where civility is challenged every day. Many teenagers, perceiving little respect in their neighborhood, feel they have to get it in whatever way they can. All too often that means through violent confrontation.

Everybody is close in drug-dealing zones, Dexter points out. And with the drop in drug prices—in 1980 a kilogram of cocaine cost $50,000; in 1993 it cost $14,000—and consequent heightened competition, many copping zones, where illegal drugs are sold, have seen increasingly violent encounters.

This talk about money gets Dexter, who is directly familiar with the fall in the price of crack, from twenty dollars to two or three dollars a "bottle," back on the subject of money: how little he has, how little teenagers in the projects actually make by selling drugs. "And now it's not too much money in the game. But people still get into it and now they make bigger [crack cocaine] bottles. A few years ago ten thousand a month was a lot of money, but today that's only a down payment on a forty-, fifty-thousand-dollar ride [car]." Dexter mentions his former crew boss, who respected him and wanted him as a partner. Dexter left the crew and drug dealing; the boss continued in the business. "Before, when I was with him, he had a Acura Integra. Now he's got a Saab 9000 and a Acura Legend."

Although traditional economic institutions have withdrawn from many urban areas, strict market forces are still at work—in the drug trade. As lower-level and blue-collar jobs disappeared, and better jobs required higher levels of education, and the quality of education in black communities fell behind, the drug trade became the only livelihood of choice, the only source of cash, for many. And to succeed in the drug trade, as Dexter and others point out, hard work and discipline are necessary. A business that apparently rejects mainstream culture at the same time embraces it: drug dealers break the law, yet their livelihood merely indicates their conforming to a larger culture of entrepreneurship and consumption.

Girls in the Projects

How do young women navigate the projects, make decisions to avoid the dangers, and discover opportunities to expand their horizons? Parents and other adults often help them, but sometimes parental approaches are very harmful and can have an effect the opposite of that intended.

Young women often find themselves in "forced" or "locked-up" situations, as Marisa tells us. Her parents, like others, do not allow their daughters to "hang out in the street and be with older boys." Marisa recounts how her mother embarrassed her when she brought a boy home so her mother could meet him before they started dating. She thought she was doing exactly what her mother would want. "I was thirteen, and this boy was sixteen. My mother came out and I introduced him to her, and she says, 'How old are you?' and he told her. She picked up his jacket and says, 'You have to leave, you're too old for my daughter.' I was so hurt that I broke down and cried. She had always told me to tell her everything and do right, but it was totally wrong for her to do that to me.

"I liked older boys because they taught me more," Marisa says. "One of my boyfriends was a dealer, and another one went to church." She feels unremitting pressure from her mother and grandmother; once, when she "disobeyed" her mother by coming home late, she was sent to Puerto Rico for a year.

Sheena, who was brought up by her grandmother in the neighborhood around the Johnson projects, appreciates the nurturing her grandmother gave her and what difference it made in her life. "My grandmother always told me, 'It's a big world out there, Sheena, and if you fall you got to pick yourself up. You are your own best friend. You have to keep yourself happy and not worry about trying to deal with negative people. People who encourage and support is what to look for, not the things and people in the street.'

"There is nothing for me to do in the street, although that was not always true. A lot of what my grandmother told me to do at certain stages of my life I didn't wanna hear about. A lot of times she told me stuff and it didn't work. It didn't work because I wasn't listening to anybody at that time. Seventeen was my worst year—I didn't wanna stay at home, nobody could tell me anything. It was like a mental thing, you know, nothing else, just being disobedient. I was just hardheaded and wanted to do devilment."

Sheena, who dropped out of high school shortly before her baby was born, sees Xiamara as a reason to "do positive things and be a positive person. I have to do it for her. When my grandmother used to tell me all these things—these dos and don'ts—I would hope she would be wrong, and then I'd go out there and mess up. Then I'd have to crawl back in and admit she was right. I knew all along in my gut she was right. You know how you get nervous when your parents say something with conviction? You know they're right, but you go out and do something they don't want you to do anyway? Well, that's what happened to me. I didn't listen, and I got pregnant. But I've learned a lot about that part of life, and all the dangers out there."

Sheena has written a poem about those dangers, and she has committed it to memory:

Who knows of the dangers lurking for me.
Who knows the stranger waiting to be: a murderer,
   a junkie, a prisoner of war, a doctor of malpractice
   or a bum on the floor.
Is that what I'm thinking deep in my mind?
Is that what can happen if we run out of time?
I'm almost out of the tunnel all weary and wet.
I'm stuck with a virus that make me sweat.
No AIDS—I'm cool—it's much worse than that,
   it's something that is an important fact.

It's I-S-O-L-, and it's worse than hell.
It's dealing with day, it's dealing with night,
  believe it or not, I'm scared of life.

Sheena is proud of her poem, written, she says, "one day when I just couldn't stop writing. I just kept writing, and then all of sudden I had that little poem." While some of the perils she records are those faced principally or exclusively by young women in her community, many are hazards to people everywhere, problems by no means limited to Sheena's social world.

Sheena counts her current boyfriend among the major influences on her, even though she has had misgivings about him. He is "great" for her, she says; "he's not into the negative stuff so many young people are into. He's older than me, and very intelligent and outgoing. He loves to improve himself and helps me to improve myself. We've been to museums together, and every night we play a one-hundred-question game. We ask each other questions, things to expand our knowledge. I want to go back to school, and my boyfriend wants me to, and just as soon as I get myself together I'll be doing that.

"My baby was very sick before, and it bothered me to the point where I couldn't do anything else. She had nothing but phlegm in her chest for months. She would get high fevers and I would take her to the hospital. It was very cold and I thought she was going to catch pneumonia. I've been through a lot of trouble. I was in a car accident last year and I had a problem with my back, so I had to deal with that. But I'm okay, and so is she. You should see her, walking and talking and everything.

"So many of my girlfriends are having problems. I feel mine are small compared to theirs. I really have nothing to complain about. They don't have anybody to take care of them. They get this romantic idea that love is somehow involved in sex with boys. I tell them that ain't happening." Perhaps Sheena exaggerates when she says further that all her friends are either having babies or on crack. Yet her comment reflects the inescapable reality of drug use and teen pregnancy in the community.

The uptown kids, growing up in poor neighborhoods in a declining city, have had to rely on sophisticated coping strategies and defense postures, sometimes of their own making. Joyce, Marcus, and Tina have been for the most part sheltered from street life; they have relied on the sponsorship of parents and other adults, on specialized instruction, and other guidance. Paco, Dexter, and Sheena, meanwhile, rely on their identities as members of drug gangs, posses, or graffiti crews. Paco went even further, and thought about ways to sell his art. His form of self-expression, like that of his peers in the projects, is but a way to cope, to maintain faith in themselves, in what might otherwise be desperate circumstances.

"Stretch thru Pain," a sketch by Paco

CHAPTER 6

Death and Escape

This chapter contains descriptions of violent acts that may be disturbing to some people. If the reader has suffered the loss of a teenage family member in a violent way, a debriefing may be in order.

"The mob crushed him after his gun didn't go off," Budd is telling Jack, who stands near a window in Terry Williams's apartment. Jack seems to be relishing the story. Terry overhears them and asks what their conversation is about, as the Writers Crew session is about to start. The subject today is death and violence.

Budd gives the appearance of a gentle, shy young man. He is known for his good looks, the care he takes with his Gumby hairstyle, and his great personal charm. These qualities contrast markedly with the brutality and desperation of his story.

As we were expanding our network of acquaintance with teenagers and young adults in the Harlem projects, a series of violent events fixed a glaring spotlight on the crisis among New

165

York City's youth. One night in the spring of 1989, groups of Latino and African-American teenagers rampaged through Manhattan's Central Park. A number of adults, most of them white and middle-class, were wounded; others were badly shaken. One, a female jogger, was brutally beaten, raped, and left for dead. A few weeks later three African-American young men were attacked in the Bensonhurst section of Brooklyn, and one was bludgeoned to death by racially enraged white men. The two events have come to symbolize the dangerous climate of violence and conflicted race relations in New York City.

In Harlem's housing projects and its older apartment house neighborhoods, these events became the subject of intense reflection and bitter debate. And not just these events, for at around the same time: Two children were abducted from a City Parks Department playground adjacent to King Towers. Two teenagers were killed in an aborted cocaine transaction in another project. One teenage boy was killed and another left comatose after a brutal episode of gang violence outside still another project. A gang of teenage girls conducted a series of needle-stabbing attacks on Manhattan's West Side. Unknown numbers of children and teenagers were victimized by parents trapped in a world of addiction or marginal involvement in the narcotics industry. Births of children addicted to cocaine and alcohol were on the rise, not only in Harlem but in many neighborhoods throughout the city.

You cannot talk to anyone in Harlem, in the projects or the surrounding neighborhoods, without hearing moving accounts of suffering, fear, and courage. Simply to lift the phone and call the police with a complaint about a narcotics sale you've witnessed requires courage, to say nothing of what it takes to organize tenants to drive out drug dealers. Nor is the situation very different in the more privileged neighborhoods around Harlem. In the projects one hears little belief in a prompt solution to the crisis. There are instead warnings that "resources are limited," with the federal deficit so high. Chances of strong initiatives from

Washington improved decidedly with the Clinton–Gore succession to leadership, but Harlem neighbors retain a healthy skepticism. The environment for adolescent development in Harlem becomes ever more risky.

Some of the boys who joined the so-called wolf packs in Central Park came from the Harlem projects we are working in. Some came from more middle-class housing. Residents of Schomburg Plaza, a middle-income complex, had been asking the police and other agencies for help in dealing with a particularly violent group of fifteen to twenty teenagers who had been terrorizing the neighborhood for months prior to the violence in Central Park. These residents were told nothing could be done because the incidents involved teenagers. The police felt teenagers in gangs were uncontrollable unless witnesses came forth to testify against them, and most residents avoid doing so. The people in Schomburg, however, believe the police didn't respond out of racism and their unwillingness to distribute justice equally in the community. "It took the rape and beating of a white woman," the residents say, to get the police to pay attention to the teenagers. Only then were their complaints about the teenagers heard.

Around this group of teenagers there coalesced a larger and more amorphous network of youths who eventually rampaged in the park. Those who were involved in the rape attack on the jogger stood trial and are serving prison sentences of lengths that do not appear to have much to do with their actual roles in the event. By law they should have received lesser sentences than they did.

A few years have passed since the incident in Central Park, and no concerted steps have been taken to address the problem of youth violence in uptown neighborhoods. The situation is getting worse. Hundreds of teenagers from poor neighborhoods all over the city rampaged through Manhattan and elsewhere on Halloween 1990. The respite of the winter months is only temporary. Episodes of shooting and violence in the schools are becoming more common, and school officials are also warning of an unprecedented epidemic of youth violence.

After some good-natured pleading from the rest of the Writers Crew, Budd agrees to read from his journal. He begins tentatively, but not at all nervously: " 'Today is the first day I really decided to record my thoughts and certain events that happen in my life. Let me start by saying that New York City is not the safest place in the world to be. So much violence, too much tension, and a hell of a lot of confusion. Today I was assaulted [in Washington Square Park] by a wolf pack, as society calls them. It's basically a group of teenagers hanging out and starting trouble for no apparent reason. As I see it, these teenagers have many problems and a lot of anger. They just misplace their anger on innocent people. These teenagers aren't aware that they're misplacing their anger, but some come to the realization of their own doing. I should know. I'm an ex-member of a wolf pack, the Madison Avenue Robo Mobsters. Anyway, I was hanging out in Washington Square Park located in Greenwich Village. I hang there practically every day. It's a place where you can go and just be yourself.' "

Budd's journal entry ends there. The Crew wants to know more about his experiences and what is on his mind. Tina gently inquires if he would mind talking about it. He agrees, takes out a brush, and brushes his wavy hair up.

"I started hanging down there because I didn't like hanging uptown. There's so much wrongdoing up here, everybody wanting to fight and profile [to say you are going to do something but with no intention of following through]. I had enough fighting, so I decided to change my way, change the way I dress. And someone introduced me to the Village. And now, there's negativity down there, but it's in a different form."

Jack asks Budd how he feels about "this wilding, wolf-pack thing. I mean, since you were part of one, what did you call yourself?"

Looking slightly surprised by the question, Budd repeats the question for himself. "What did we call ourselves? Well, we called ourselves a mob. We called ourselves the Madison Avenue Robo Mobsters because we lived in the projects on that Avenue. We started off with four members—Gadget, Stick, Blade, and me. And we just hung out, and there was a lot of profiling. All of us knew martial arts and also took boxing, so we were known as good fighters. If someone wanted to test us, we wouldn't back down, we would fight one-on-one. And then people really started admiring us. They would say, 'I want to hang out with Budd, you know, he's so cool. He can fight so well. You should have seen him beat up that guy.' At that time, I thought I was cool and, Yeah, I'm Budd, you don't mess with me. For a while I had a height complex, because I was short.

"So it started off with four," Budd continues. "And then it blew up, ten, twenty, thirty, and at the end of last summer the gang had another chapter. It was called the Madison Avenue Robo Mobster Association. These kids were from Brooklyn and places like that. It was widespread, it got real big, at least a hundred. And after that, when the third association was put together, the Baby Madison Avenue Robo Mobsters—these were kids twelve to fourteen—I left the mob. That's when I just faded away. We'd always say there were no leaders, you know. But as you can see, we had the leadership.

"Gadget—he's a big short husky guy—was our leader. Best boxer ever out in the street. It's been a long time since he lost a fight. He's just so wide and so big, and people fear muscle. Then we had Stick, the tall one. Everyone else in the association was short. Stick was the tallest one, and kind of heavy. And he also boxed. Me, I'm a martial artist, and I knew how to fight. Basically I thought with my head. Gadget didn't think. He just did it. He was brutal. Stick followed Gadget. When Gadget wasn't around, everyone listened to Stick. If Stick wasn't around, they would listen to me."

The Writers Crew waits for Budd to tell about the things the gang did and, more important, why they did them. Marisa speaks for the others when she asks, "Why were you so into hurting people?"

Budd answers by describing the gang's solidarity: "We hung out together. We went to parties together. We used to drink together." And when he and his friends hung out together, they "talked a lot of garbage and nonsense, and waited for somebody to make a wrong move and give us a wrong look or walk through our block. And they didn't live there, and we would beat 'em up and profile. We would love it, you know?"

"What would cause you to do that?" Sheena wonders.

Budd hesitates for a moment. "Well, we did some pretty fucked-up things to people, but we also helped some people." On the bad side, he says, when the gang saw somebody "come through the projects, we would say, like, 'Who the hell does this guy think he is?' One of us would say that out loud so the person would look back or he and his friends would look back and say, 'What?' And we would walk up to him, and boom, bash, bam, boom. Basically it would start off like that. Then on the good side, it was like when we were first hanging out. If an old lady got robbed, we would help out. We would chase the guy and beat him down and get the money back. Then it became a game after a while, a Robin Hood–type game. That went on for about two years. Then you got new jacks [kids in the projects] in the group, and they felt they had to prove something, so we'd do crazy shit."

Budd takes a deep breath, as he gears up to talk about one of the more startling events in his young life. It happened when he was still a member of the Mobsters, and he says it changed his mind and opened a new chapter in his life. He knew how much he had to leave the projects. "This happened at something we call a jam session, a slammin' jam [party], outside in one of the school yards on 100th Street. Everybody is hanging out. The girls are all there, and we be drinking and be drunk as ever. I had already begun to sort of fade away from the group, but then I would occasionally come back and hang out. Every time a party is thrown there's a fight, and it has to be the Madison Avenue Robo Mobsters in it, you know. So there was some guys, with two Mad Ave Mob Girls, and these dudes were profiling. They were from downtown, Alphabet City, Avenue A, B, spots like that. So Gadget dissed one of them by going up to one of the girls and grabbing her, and saying 'Come here, baby' and trying to kiss on her. And the kid whose girl it was, says, 'Yo! Man, what you doing?' Gadget told him, 'Shut up and mind your business, or I'm gonna drop you.' We had this signal, like a whistle, and when that whistle goes, you know there's trouble. So that whistle was made and everyone's head turns, boom, straight toward the sound. Gadget was standing in the kid's face. And the kid's friend was on the side, saying, 'Calm down, calm down.' And the mob is like, 'Wolf, wolf, wolf.' Gadget snuffed the kid, boom, and when Gadget hits somebody, it's very rare that the person stands up—he knocks people out. He knocked the kid out, right? And then the other kid pulled out a gun and pointed it at Gadget and pulled the trigger—click, click, click, click. But nothing came out. He didn't have the clip inside the gun. He had it inside his pocket. I don't know why, I guess it was just a reaction. Everything got quiet for a moment. And then Gadget hit him, boom. And everybody hit him, boom. And the kid that was knocked out, everybody was stomping on him. There was no need for him to be kicked anymore. They continued to beat him. His balls, testicles, they were squashed. They were just gone.

"Ever since that day," Budd says, curling his lip to one side of his mouth, "I was like, Arrgh. And I faded away from those guys. I started hanging out with my female friends. I would try to avoid those guys, and they're like, 'Yo, Budd man, what's up? You don't hang out with us no more.' I'm like, 'I'm busy, I'm busy.' And they go, 'Come on, man, for old time's sake. Old time's sake.' And it was cool sometimes, 'cause sometimes we'd go to a place, like in Central Park, have a couple of beers. There'd be a whole bunch of us. And we sang songs that we wrote. You know, I write songs," he says, with a glint in his eye.

"And this other kid, Pedro, writes songs. So we'd sing. We would be drunk out of our minds and we would just sing and sing and sing, and it would be so much fun. Sometimes I lay down in bed and I think about the times that we hung out and we just sang. And I also thought a lot about those two kids. They were in the hospital for a while. I heard that one died and the other one was in a coma for a long time. So the State found out. Their friends found out. And family members found out where we lived, uptown Madison Avenue, and what the name of our mob was. So they came around constantly in jeeps looking for us."

One day, Budd recounts, a strange car pulled up to his group, all of whose members were "strapped"—carrying guns— at the time. Someone in the car called for Stick, insults were traded, and suddenly an erratic, deeply troubled Puerto Rican boy in Budd's gang shot a person in the car in the head. More shots were fired before everyone ran. A week later the boy who fired the fatal shot was in jail and Stick was on the run as a fugitive.

The mood in the room turns somber. Everyone knows people who have died in the past two or three years, often in violent episodes involving guns. Naturally the discussion centers on why murderous force is so common. Budd says that while using knives or guns was once thought of as cowardice, now everyone relies on weapons. "It's not cowardice anymore. It's mob stuff to have guns. These are the 1990s and this is the new tech, and you go for it. This is how you do things. Maybe back in '79 you might have been putting up your hands. Now"—he raises his hand and points his finger—"it's all about boom, boom, boom."

Terry asks Budd where the guns come from and how easily can they be obtained. "Down south," he answers, his forehead stiffening as if a bad thought were racing through his mind. "Derain, who is one of the new mob leaders now, has access to guns down south. So he drives down with drugs and drives back with guns. So that's how they get guns. It's real easy to get them. They be bringing back Tecs, deuce-fives [.25-caliber guns], nines [nine-millimeters], Mac10s, Uzis. You name it, they got it. And these be kids my age, like seventeen, eighteen, nineteen. Gadget's only seventeen."

Budd goes on to talk about the Robo Mobsters and drug dealing. Though it is not primarily a drug-dealing crew, many of its members have—like so many local boys—had at least passing involvement with the crack business, as a way of making sneaker money.

Girls, Skeezers, and Crack Money

Attention turns to the girls who spend time with the Robo Mobsters. What goes on between them and the boys? Do the boys feel the need to do illegal acts to impress the girls? Budd doesn't know where to begin, but Dexter has something to say: "I wrote this bit in my journal that's sort of about the thing with the girls. 'I wanna see Kid Capri. I wanna see him at the party because I know they got girls there. The party is at nine o'clock. But the last time I saw a bunch of girls there they wanted to go to a park. They had two blunts. Kid Capri had it overflowing at the 118th Street gym between Fifth and Lenox. The sidewalk had hundreds and it was jampacked inside. The cops coming down telling everybody to get out of the street.

" 'I saw this girl and said, "What's up? What's up? What's up?" She walked right past me. So I said, "Yo, bitch, you played yourself." Then when I saw them later they came over to me and said they wanted some smoke and we went to three spots and still couldn't find no smoke. I was gonna beep my man because these bitches started acting all ill and shit.

" 'Then we go back to 118th Street and as soon as we got there something jumped off in the middle of the party. Somebody started shooting up in there. So me and my partner standing outside, and two his partners wanna get naughty wid a forty [forty-ounce malt beer] and some Cisco [liquid crack], but I ain't wid that. I meet this other kid who got a cordless [phone] and he's frontin' [pretending] on me. He's profilin' for the ladies, and you know that's how fights get started. So I told him to be cool and jetted. But you know, it all boils down to the pussy, the exchange.

" 'Everybody who go to the parties is part of the exchange or they want to be part of the exchange. It's like a scene that you know. There ain't all that much real feeling there. It's a thing that will eventually lead to sex. Now in the meantime, the bitches they be looking for a ride, some money, some drugs, the best-looking men, the boys with cars and gold, and niggers with fades [special haircuts].

" 'The boys be looking for brown-skinned or light-skinned girls with big earrings and big butts. The girls be looking for respect too, sometimes. They don't feel they're treated right by males so they compete and compensate. They be striving to get to the top of their game too. They be gaming to get the dick and step off just like the males be gaming to get the pussy and step off.' "

Dexter's reading—with some improvisation—draws laughter, and shouts of both derision and support from the Crew. But everyone is still waiting for Budd to take up the subject of girls and the Madison Avenue mob. Budd looks at the floor, then takes out his comb and strokes his wavy hair a few times. He puts the comb back into his pocket without removing his gaze from the floor.

"Girls. Yeah, the boys be frontin' for the girls all the time. Because, you know, if you don't have any money up here, if you don't have any chunky jewelry on, some slammin' wheels, you're nobody. Oh, you're cute, you know—that's how they see me—but you ain't got no money. Then again, they got them skeezers." The other crew members exchange knowing glances as Budd broaches this subject. Originally the term "skeezers" applied to good-looking young women who used their charms with successful drug dealers. More recently the word has come to refer to women who trade sex for crack, especially low-down, addicted women, also known as "crack bitches."

"Yeah, they got skeezers," Budd repeats, "but I don't waste time with them. I don't date any girls in my area either. I associate with them, but I don't mess with them. Skeezers are, I think, really evil. I wouldn't call my sister a skeezer, but there are rumors that she's a potential one." He laughs as embarrassed glances shoot around the room: some of the Crew know Budd's sister, who associates with drug crew members. "I shouldn't call her a skeezer, but I think she's a compulsive liar. [He's joking.] She's fifteen years old and hangs out with the crowd I used to hang out with. That's why she's profiling. Everybody knows her as 'Budd's sister,' so she's got that respect. People say, 'Don't talk to her, don't touch her, because Budd will come and get you.' So it's like that. She knows I was part of that gang, and she has been able to use that. She spreads rumors, and people come back to me, like, Your sister said this and that, and you're going to beat up this and that person. But I don't fight anymore."

Budd looks convincing when he says these words. He continues to discuss his sister: "My sister is very pretty. I think she's just profiling. I tell her not to hang out with that crowd, and I try not to yell at her. I don't want her to fear me, but I say, 'Yo, sit down, all right?' and I tell her what's on my mind. I try not to make her feel so bad, you know, just let her know I'm serious. I tell her, 'I'll punch you upside your head if you don't get straight.' " Budd laughs.

The subject of skeezers begs for more discussion, but perhaps it is too sensitive a topic for the group to explore further with any confidence. They know the AIDS epidemic has claimed the lives of too many of the once vivacious young women who frequented the drug crews; at first the starlets of their own show, they became "buffers," professional fellatio artists, then skeezers. AIDS is the most prevalent cause of death for these women.

Too many get into trouble with the police before they realize they are not immortal and must find help to escape.

For Budd and many teenagers like him, the most dangerous time of life is the period between twelve and eighteen years of age, which might be referred to as the "immortality stage," when teenagers have no comprehension of their own ability to die. In New York City, 50 children under the age of seventeen were shot to death in 1992. More than 270 were wounded by gunfire. About 260 under age sixteen were arrested and turned over to family court for possessing weapons, and many have been remanded to the adult criminal justice system. The violence around the cocaine crews in the projects usually occurs as a result of their attempts to protect their turf within the projects. Of all the special areas teenagers colonize, by far the most common is the street corner.

Jack, who has a history of violence at home, in his relationships with women, and on the job, reads from his journal: " 'I'm getting tired of niggers [bad people] trying to dis me, word. I try to be as straight up with people as I can, and some people just don't know how to deal with that. Last week I had an incident that took place at Sweet Basil's [a Greenwich Village jazz club]. Maybe I fucked up, but at this point I'm really not concerned because I'm not that uncomfortable with what I did. I went down to Sweet Basil's as an expected guest with a couple of my homeboys. Now, when we got to the door, this maître d' started acting funny. I felt that he was bugging because we're a couple of young black men and he may have felt that we were going to somehow make the other patrons feel uncomfortable. See, he fucked up when he pushed me as I turned around to walk away from the front door. That's when I just punched this mother-fucker in the mouth over some stupid shit. That shit felt so good that I wanted to finish him off, but you know the scenario, the police would have come and thrown my black ass in jail.' "

Jack isn't the only Crew member at this session who has been having heavy thoughts. Sheena has been worried too, as she expressed to Terry sometime earlier outside her building. Sheena seems always to have a warm, even disposition, so it was unusual to see her distressed that day. But it was clear why early in the conversation.

"I'm pregnant again," Sheena said without blinking. "I've been sick and had some migraine headaches." She took out a baby bottle and gave it to an anxious Xiamara. "I get weak and catch colds real easy now. If I had the money I'd get an abortion. I don't want to have another baby." She talked about what an abortion would mean and how much it would cost; she said she didn't have much moral support from her boyfriend.

Now, as she listens to Budd and others in the Crew talk about danger and death, Sheena is thinking even more about how much she wants an abortion, how she can not bring another baby into her life. But where will she get the money? Usually an eager contributor to Crew discussions, she sits quietly, lost in the dreadful associations all these stories of death conjure in her mind.

Sheena does not attend the next few Writers Crew meetings; she calls only once during this time. This behavior is unlike her. Then, in a letter to Terry Williams, she explains that because of personal problems she hasn't been able to attend Crew meetings. (During this time she has an abortion.) One night around eleven, while driving along Adam Clayton Powell, Jr., Boulevard, Terry sees Sheena and Xiamara crossing the street. He asks why she is out at that hour with her baby. "I just wanted to get out of them damn projects for a while," Sheena answers. "Xiamara can't sleep in her room without crying." The baby, Terry notices, is well dressed, wearing apparently new shoes and clothes; at that time of night she is hardly talkative, but Sheena says she is hungry.

Poor families obviously do not have the support networks of middle- and higher-income families, so young people look for ways out, ways around and beyond their neighborhood. We cannot understand or appreciate their resilience until we recognize the hardship, risk, and trauma they have had to endure. We must know what obstacles they face; how much racism they encounter; what degree of violence they experience, in the home and out; how many deaths they witness; how much and what kind of personal rejection they have had in their lives. Only then will we comprehend their struggle, and the significance of their survival and, indeed, their victory.

At another session of the Writers Crew, Budd is again the center of attention. Talking about the shooting and the kid's death took a great deal of courage on his part; he is opening up to the Crew. Today the group wants to hear him talk about his deciding to leave the neighborhood. Budd came from a good family in the projects but he fell in with a bad street element; he is beginning to find a new life downtown, in the Village. Does he think this change is a logical development, or is it extraordinary?

"I left," Budd says slowly, "because of what I seen that we done to people. We hurt people real bad. We stabbed people. We shot people. We stomped people. We hurt people just to see someone laying there bleeding, you know. It's like, Oh man, what if that was me? I knew that could be me. I got a [police] record now. And that just messed up my life. Then I got arrested again. I got arrested three times, and it's like, Oh man, I got to chill out, you know. My mom is telling me, Chill out. And like, I wasn't really listening. Until the last time I got arrested. I'm on five years' probation now. So it's chill out for real, just don't hang out with that crowd anymore. What goes around comes around."

Budd says that he realized he was marked for death unless he weaned himself from the Robo Mobsters. He needed new friends, new places of interest. The violence he engaged in with the Robo Mobsters left an indelible impression on him; in fact, it brought him to change his life. During his early teens, Budd felt immortal; he did not recognize the dangers surrounding him. By the time he was seventeen, however, he had seen enough to realize his mortality.

As Budd sits silently, Dexter asks if he might say a few words about a similar change in his life. He realized that he could—and moreover, had to—avoid a premature turn with death after he was arrested and sentenced to five years' probation for his involvement in drug dealing. But it was the death of street buddies that really brought home the idea of his own mortality. Critical in his dealing with this reality was finding people ready to lend him a hand and speak for him.

Someone to Speak for Him

One night not long after this Writer's Crew meeting, Terry Williams receives a call from Dexter. His voice is breathless with anxiety. A friend of his—street name "Chronic"—has been arrested on a murder charge. Dexter goes on to tell Terry as much as he knows: "There was conflict between Chronic and this man. They was on the street, and the man had a gun. Nobody knew he had a gun, though. At first he was calling Chronic, so Chronic goes up to him, and then he pulled out a gun. Chronic ran. The guy started chasing him. Then Chronic's friends say, We can't have this. So they pulled up and they shot him. Oh, they had beat the guy with a bat, I think it was."

Terry asks for some specifics. How old is Chronic? How old was the other man?

Chronic is twenty-one, the other man was older, Dexter says. He adds that Chronic has been in jail for four days now. "The cops was looking for Chronic, they saw him. Chronic went to the precinct, gave himself in, like, 'Why are they looking for me?' They kept him and say, 'Well, you've been charged with murder.' People saying they seen him. They did, I guess. They say they seen the man in conflict there with Chronic, they seen him and Chronic arguing. Then later on they see that the man is dead. So they said Chronic killed him.

"Chronic left the block?" Terry asks.

"Yeah, he ran," says Dexter.

"So there are no witnesses to say they saw him actually shoot the guy?"

"There was two witnesses saying that he didn't do it. And I heard there's also witnesses saying that he did. People say that he did it. There's two dudes said that he did shoot and that he did shoot them."

Has Chronic been in trouble before? Terry wonders. Dexter isn't sure. Has he been involved in drug dealing? On this Dexter is certain: "No, he wasn't, no, no."

"So why were Chronic's friends beating this guy?" Terry asks. "Do you know?"

"No, I don't," Dexter says. "There be so many people involved with it that you really don't know who did what. When it's all over with, everybody scattered, go different ways." The police, as a result, "didn't get everybody that was with it."

"So what do you want me to do?" Terry asks now.

"Well, his grandmom was talking about where she was going to get a lawyer for him. I wanted to talk to you first so that she don't go out and spend all the money. I felt like if I talk to you, at least she could be referred to somebody instead of just going out looking for a lawyer. Because the man is innocent. He had something to do wid it, but he didn't do the killing. This is what his brother told me. You see, I wasn't there. I just know what he told me."

"Well, whether he's innocent or guilty, he needs good counsel. He needs a good lawyer."

"Somebody to speak for him," Dexter says.

"Yeah," Terry concurs, "somebody to speak for him."

Terry eventually puts Dexter's friend in touch with a fine criminal lawyer with whom he had worked in the past, but equally important to Dexter was the fact that he knew he had someone, and perhaps more than just one person, to turn to for help. There were people who could talk for him, people outside his extremely resource-limited family circle who believed in him and were willing to help him.

Dexter is forming the trust needed to reach out to others. Budd too seems to be developing trust in others; he opens up with the Writers Crew, even though he has joined the group only tentatively. He goes into intimate aspects of his relationship with his mother and his stepfather, both of whom, he feels, talk "at him" not with him. He talks about his fears for his sister, and how difficult it was for him to move out of his family's project apartment and live alone at age eighteen. He lasted almost a year on his own, but there was too much pressure to work and he made too little money to pay rent. When his roommate left, Budd was forced to leave the apartment. He was also under pressure from drug-dealing friends who wanted him to join their crew.

Fellow Writers Crew members contribute stories of their own experiences, and a sense of sharing and a camaraderie is established. It is a great relief for Budd to talk about the things that plague him, and to hear that others have problems too— and perhaps advice for him as well. For Sheena the Crew sessions are a talking cure: she can speak freely about anything, about her father and her brother for instance. A powerful attraction of the Crew for all its members is the chance to express themselves candidly with adults who are interested in them as individuals and want to spend time with them; who think they have talent and want to cultivate it, through their writing for example; and who seem to understand their situation, and even respect their need for "sneaker money."

Escape in Two Worlds:
Home Versus Street

Terry Williams heads south from his building one afternoon, on his way to meet Dexter for lunch. As soon as he reaches Dexter's block he hears what sounds like gunfire from a nine-millimeter. Kids on the corner, familiar with the noise, turn toward it.

Dexter, back from a job downtown, approaches. "Wanna meet my friend?" he says, then introduces Snoopie, a muscular, ruggedly handsome young man with a gold-capped tooth. He has just returned from the upstate prison where he has spent the last two years, one of 62,000 inmates in the New York state prison system.

In the old days, on many a street corner, one might have seen men with conked hair, talking loudly but saying nothing, drinking beer—all to the consternation of white-dressed women going home from church. These were street-wise men, who fought the police and punished anybody who crossed them; they personified the "bad nigger" element in street life. Snoopie is like them. He's a tough kid, one of the toughest. He is the first to admit that he is not interested in becoming a model citizen, or writing for that matter. He wants to make money and rap.

Snoopie's account of his experiences contrasts strikingly with the belief that poor youths see prison as a way to prove their manhood. "I used to be scared when I was upstate [in prison]. The kids out there my age—eighteen, nineteen—they always talk about jail like it's a vacation. But jails now is different. Check out the way they put me in solitary one time for thirty days, right? Suppose they start putting niggers in there for longer—you know, you do your entire time in solitary, you just sit in your cell, you don't get TV or nothing. That would drive you crazy. You go mad in there. You do bugging-out stuff. You do two years of that and you've got to change. You come out: 'Well, I'm going back and getting a job. Nine to five all day, all year.'

"The police upstate was nothing but white people, and they hated the blacks. There was a fight in my dorm one day. We was in the laundry room, where they go to fight because the police won't see. They jumped this kid because he was from another dorm and he came down to run things in my dorm. And there was a punky kid they started jumping. They bust him in the head. He pressed a button and the police came, and when they came,

everybody in the dorm was getting hit. They was hitting everybody even if you wasn't involved, even if you was asleep. They
woke everybody up. They strip-searched everybody and
checked lockers and all that. Everybody was getting written up.
They sent me and three other dudes to the box because I had a
lock. They caught me with the lock"—which, Snoopie maintains, he did not use as a weapon—"they threw me in the box
for thirty days."

Snoopie was in solitary confinement for a total of six
months during his prison stay. He admits he was a difficult
prisoner. "I used to be the ass-kicker sometimes. They started
sending letters to my mother. They tried to scare me up. They
said they was going to send me to a max joint like Attica. That's
when I said no, that's when I slowed down. Those guys will kill
you quick up there, for cigarettes and all of that." Snoopie was
even robbed of money shortly before his release but chose to
keep silent about it.

"Kids say, 'When I get there [in jail], I'll do this or that. I'm
going to hang loose.' But when you get there it changes, and
you're a whole different person. You've got to be a man, you've
got to be strong. I got locked up three times. When I first got
locked up I was scared to death. I said, 'Yo, it's either me or
them, man. They ain't getting me.' I went in there with the
attitude, 'Ain't nobody messing with me. I'll stay to myself. If
somebody want to try me I just have to get wild, get all crazy,
man.' After three fights, I gained a little respect and they started
to see me as cool."

Even with the threat of jail, Snoopie says, many kids see
only the material gain possible—"the jeeps, the money, and all
that. You could get locked up for five years for being caught with
drugs, but you see somebody selling drugs and all of this stuff
they got, gold, jeeps. If you ain't got caught yet, you say, 'I'm
going to try it. And hopefully, I'll be careful.' " And bam, Snoopie says, the same thing happens to you as has happened to the
many others now in jail.

Yet the reality is more sobering than what Snoopie suggests.

The United States has lost the will to feed, clothe, house, educate, and otherwise care for all of its citizens, especially the poor. Prisons are nothing more than temporary holding pens for a disposable population, one not needed in the new global labor market. Crime, welfare, and homelessness are temporarily "eliminated" in one fell swoop by local, state, and federal drug laws that sentence people with the least options and fewest resources to long prison terms. Whatever their intent or origin—and because drug dealing is a major problem of inner cities—such drug laws are in effect anti-urban laws.

Despite such laws, there is that one strong motivation which seems to outweigh the risks: "The money is what all of us want," Dexter says. "We all do it for the money, fast money." Dexter mentions also a conceptual motivation—"A lot of people do it with that attitude of not getting caught"—and Snoopie proposes popularity as a reason for some people to turn to drug dealing, yet he too understands the prime motive: "Money, money, is the most important thing for all these kids. You see your mom work hard all her life, barely making anything. Then you get a chance to go out here [and sell drugs], and your mother don't have to work. She could sleep all day, and have anything, and you could do her whole apartment over." Snoopie himself, when he sold drugs, used to buy $550 shoes. "You can go up in Gucci's and spend $3,000. I can't do that now. I'd love to do it."

"I don't think kids and people in general sell drugs because they want to kill off their own people," Snoopie says. "You've got a lot of drug dealers that do things for kids in the community. Like this guy around here, one of the big ones—I mean, yachts and everything. He's legal now, and in the summertime he takes kids from the neighborhood to Atlantic City and Great Adventures [a New Jersey amusement park], even to Florida. He does stuff like that for people. You know, he's really good."

Snoopie, like Dexter, is trying to change his way of life, after his drug dealing and his problems with the law. He is the classic good kid gone bad, now seeking to go good again. His type of resilience is particularly important in understanding a crucial point about black adolescent experience: Resilience is much harder to achieve in an environment such as Snoopie's than in the mainstream culture, and it entails different risks and rewards. Project kids reach a point at which they are willing to do better, or at least willing to try. This desire to be good citizens, to do well by society, can occur anytime in their adolescent lives.

Snoopie remembers scrambling, or dealing, for about three years. "It wasn't every day. I'd do it until I'd get a certain amount of money, maybe $2,000. Then I'd stop. I'd chill, spend some, pay back my people, then start again. I never got caught for drugs. I went to jail for fighting, assault. I had a bad attitude. When I was in jail I saw this police guy that walks around these projects. He knew me because we used to shoot dice, and he said, 'What are you here for?' Then he said to his partner, 'You didn't find no drugs on him? Check him, because he might have drugs. You know he was a drug dealer.' I told him I wasn't no drug dealer. I told him he better watch his mouth and mind who he's talking to. I talk to the police the same way they talk to me. If they treat me like a dog, man, I'm going to talk to them that way. I go to that school of respect: You talk to me with respect, you get respect. You start talking to me because I'm locked up, you think I'm a dog, I give you no respect. The only thing you can talk to me about now is freedom of speech, because I could say what I want. I let the police, the [corrections officers] know I ain't fooling."

Now, after leaving prison, Snoopie has begun his journey out of what he calls "negative thinking." He wants "to do better with life. I needed some time off from myself. I was mad at the world." He is seeking a "safe place," away from poverty, hardship, drug dealing. So far he is succeeding.

"I like rap. And that's all I do is rap. My mother says that's good, as long as I stay out of trouble. I'm going down south soon, and they got a studio a ten-minute drive from where I'm going.

I suppose I'll try to get into that studio." Snoopie goes on to describe his method: "I hear a beat, or think of it, and then make lines up off the top of my head. I don't listen to nothing else. My mother would play slow records and try to get me to listen, and I'd get out of the house. I'm basically a raphead."

Snoopie first gained praise for his accomplished technique from his friends in the street. "Everybody used to tell me I should make a record. They say I'm wasting all my talent in the street. They say I'm out robbing but I won't go to a studio or nothing. They told me every time I said a rhyme I should write it down. I said I'd have to walk around every day with a pen and a pad, because I be rhyming all the time. I could be talking and then start rapping, and they be like, 'You be bonky, man.' I rap about anything."

Budd Becomes a Bangee Boy

Budd leaves the projects and goes downtown to the Village every chance he gets. He has become a "bangee boy," a term used by gays for "lowlife." In the clubs where the action is, Budd dances to house music and has taken up voguing, a stylized mimicking of modeling poses incorporated into dance. He and friends who share his interests have formed a crew. "We hang out, and our people are essentially club kids," he says. "We be doing all the latest dances, inventing moves and acting crazy." The clubs are not a completely free world, however. "You won't believe the discrimination that goes on. B-boys [Brooklyn boys] get dissed all the time because of the 'right mix' bullshit" that happens as a result of door policy: Club doormen select who gets in the clubs, and on any given night they decide how many men and how many women, how many gays and how many straights, and of course how many blacks and how many whites.

And the criteria get more subtle than that. "Listen," Budd says, "they will not let certain black men or women in these clubs if they dressed like B-boys or B-girls, you know, with big earrings and gold chains. Now this shit is out, because what the uptown girls and the Brooklyn boys be saying is, 'I have money, look at my gold earrings, look at my gold neck chain.' The people downtown say that's just poor-man's gold, inner-city earrings. The real fucked-up part is that these are the brothers and sisters who make the K-U-L-C-H-U-R, and they can't even get into the clubs to enjoy the music, the sounds they created. They talk about we got to grow up—this whole society got to grow up."

Greenwich Village has not always been a mecca for the different and the marginalized. It certainly has not been the place where people of color have escaped discrimination. Years ago it was not uncommon for blacks to find it difficult to rent apartments and attend events in the Village. Time has passed yet racism persists. Incidents of discrimination based on race, class, and gender occur in the clubs as Budd described, but not only there.

Dexter's Dilemma

On one of the coldest nights of the year, Dexter calls Bill Kornblum with the news that he has been thrown out of his apartment. Bill calls Terry and an hour later Dexter is knocking on his door. He enters Terry's apartment and sits dejectedly, asking what he should do. "My mother doesn't understand me," Dexter says. "I don't think she understands what black males have to go through out here." Many parents in and out of the projects have a difficult time with their teenage children, and the story of Mrs. Wells and Dexter is in many ways typical.

Mrs. Wells offers her assessment of the situation to Terry

over the phone. "I told him he can stay with me if he respects me. The little money he's making now is going to his head. He says he wants to be an adult, but he should also act like an adult." Her voice is strong and clear, and although she is reluctant to show it, she is angry. She is also frustrated by contradictory feelings of wanting Dexter to act like a man—"after all, he's eighteen now"—and not wanting him to be truly independent. She wants to maintain control over his life and reap whatever good might derive from his talent. "He is not responsible yet," she asserts. "He has the privilege of a rent-free apartment here, but money is not the issue here. It's more like lack of communication. He doesn't communicate with me. He has an attitude problem. I ask him a simple question and he snaps at me. He's basically irresponsible. That's why all this talk about getting him an apartment is silly—how is he gonna pay for an apartment?"

Mrs. Wells sees her son growing up but doesn't understand his behavior. "He's so secretive, and I don't know what's going in his life. He doesn't talk to me. I don't know where he goes or what he does or who his friends are. All I know is who he's gonna run to for bail when he's in trouble. That's me, that's all. He thinks because I have a little money I should give it to him."

On his side, Dexter explains: "I never tell her anything because she favors my little brother over me. Listen to this and tell me what you think. My other friends say pretty much the same thing. Chronic says his mom charges him five dollars every time he eats at her house. Now what kinda stuff is that?"

Mrs. Wells reasons: "He lives here rent-free and doesn't do anything. All he does is make phone calls to his friends. Phone calls I have to pay for. He makes more calls than I do." She soon goes to the heart of the struggle: "He wants to be the man of the house, and I don't want him to be."

There is some contradiction in her talk. She has told Dexter to be a man, to go out and look for a job. But at the same time, she doesn't want him completely out of her control. Frustrated by what independence he does have, she wants him out of the apartment. "I put my life on hold for him for eighteen years," she says. "I want some respect. He's been an expensive thing to have around. I've had to pay for everything with him for so long that I feel he needs to help me out now. I want him to get a taste of life. I know it's cold out there tonight, but he needs to learn a lesson."

She adds that "he's a bad influence on my little boy, and I don't want to keep telling him not to say and do things around the boy." When Dexter was arrested for being part of a cocaine crew, Mrs. Wells continues, "who do you think had to bail him out? Well, he hangs out twenty-four hours a day in the street, and anybody who hangs out all that time is bound to get into trouble. I'm not worried about him when I ask him to leave, because he's got aunts who wouldn't let him stay in the street. I'm upset at him because he don't think before he talks. He didn't tell you what he did to me, did he?"

She seems surprised when Terry tells her Dexter did tell him: He pushed her after she hit him with an ashtray, and she called the police. "Well," she goes on, "he just thinks he can walk in here and do what he has been doing all along, but he can't."

Terry asks if she will allow Dexter to come back home. She says she will, but only if he will apologize to her. Dexter agrees to. "You got any carfare?" he asks, looking less defeated. Terry gives him a few dollars for a cab, and Dexter leaves gratefully: "I'll pay you back, T. You know one day I'll pay you back." Dexter goes to the subway, and after several hours spent riding the trains, drinking beer, and getting into a fistfight, he goes home to his mother's.

Parents in public housing usually understand far better than outsiders the risks their children face. Many such parents can sympathize with Mrs. Wells and have felt frustration like hers, although they may handle their own situation differently. Too often parents in public housing must calm children afraid to go to school because they are being bullied, or pressured to join one or another gang, or scorned by classmates for not having "proper" clothes or sneakers. Too often these parents must hope that their teenage children are not among those congregating in trouble spots in the neighborhood. But being aware of the risks—and temporarily calming fears or hoping for the best—does not necessarily mean doing something about them. Many parents are left to grope for real, lasting solutions.

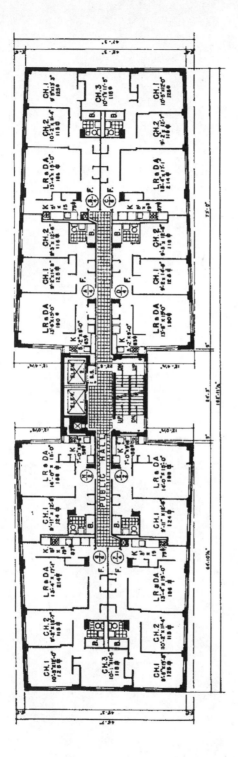

**New York City Housing Authority floor plan.
Dexter's apartment is at lower left.**

CHAPTER 7

Home
in the Projects

As he returned home once from a Writers Crew meeting, Dexter saw three Puerto Rican teenagers selling crack near the corner *grocería*. He passed them cursing under his breath, disgusted at the gall of these kids moving into *his* turf. His possessiveness was unwarranted; he didn't really control anything. He entered his building and walked down the typical narrow project hallway with its dull green walls and gray linoleum floor, and saw several deals going down there as well. Four kids in sneakers moved quickly aside so he could pass. They never moved that swiftly for most others, even adults, but street word had it that Dexter was good people. He was not sure why. Perhaps it was the way he carried himself, with a calm self-assurance, a piercing gaze, and an ability to know when and how to speak or act. At any rate, he knew how to talk to the police.

"That's it," he mumbled to himself as he walked past.

As he relates afterward, once in his apartment Dexter decided to call the police "and tell 'em a kid in my building has a gun. This is so they would send a bunch of them five-o [police] motherfuckers over here and bust these punks. I was sick of this shit. But when I'm on the phone they wanna know what kind of gun it is. I figure they trying to trace this call, so I just tell 'em some kid's got a gun and hang up.

"I wait and nothing happens, so I go downstairs to see what's up. I'm wearing my hoody, black jeans, combat boots, and looking chill. And as I'm walking down the block, five-o rolls up on *me* and ask where I'm going. I say, 'To the store,' and they say, 'What's your name? Show some ID.' The big cop on the passenger side says, 'Are you packing any weapons?' And I say no. And then it hits me: These motherfuckers think I'm the one who got *the* gun. I say, 'Listen, I live here.' And they don't wanna hear that, see. They tell me to take my hands out of my pockets. They get outta the car, and one is a woman and she's in my face and pushes me. I say, 'Why y'all fucking wid me?' This get 'em mad, and we get into a shuffle and they take me to the precinct. When we get there the woman cop tells me to just be cool and don't embarrass her and I'll be outta there in a few minutes. When I go to this room they laughing and saying I look like Ice Cube, and they let me go."

Dexter takes his hands out of his pockets and gestures for emphasis. He's relishing the absurdity of the story. "I said to myself, 'Oh, shit! This is fucked up.' I was sweating bullets."

Dexter is in his mother's apartment, and he goes into her bedroom to gather loose change from the dresser. The room is nicely furnished, with both telephone and television, and its double bed is covered by a bright spread. The other bedroom, which Dexter shares with his brother, is small and gives neither of them any privacy. Dexter now goes into the living room, at some thirteen by fifteen feet about average size for the projects, and into the kitchen. When he opens the refrigerator, his brother warns him not to eat anything—or "I'll tell Mother." Dexter shuts the refrigerator door angrily; he would like to hit his brother, but he knows the consequences might be banishment from the apartment. He walks through the apartment, its walls bare save for a poster of a black child with a large tear coming from his eyes, and goes out; he heads toward Marisa's apartment in the Johnson projects.

The projects can be an oasis from the rest of the neighborhood. Street noises are blunted and quiet relief can be had for a time inside project borders. Though the homes of project kids may be cramped and bare, those spatial dimensions are not important; what counts is the individual's ability to reach out into the world beyond and strive for new possibilities. Sometimes adolescents succeed, and win approval for their actions; at other times they fail.

The Johnson project comprises ten twenty-story red brick buildings. These buildings and many like them house more people than the surrounding area, mainly because most other buildings in the area are empty. Apartments outside the projects often have higher rents than those in the projects, where the average rent is $350 dollars a month. While the rooms are not spacious, they are adequate for a small family or for a family with young children.

People in the neighborhood wait for years to get into the projects; admission is even harder these days, because new arrivals who double up with tenants take apartments immediately after they are vacant. People like living in project apartments because the buildings are solid and well kept. Although there are complaints, most of the buildings are better maintained than adjacent private houses.

The quality of life within a specific complex depends on a combination of factors, including sensitivity of management, and the residents' own standards. "We don't allow no drug dealing in this complex," Dexter says of where he lives. "I know it looks like I'm betraying something, but if you don't do it this way, pretty soon we won't have no building. I've been talking to some of these kids to get them straight, but every day it seems some new players be out here."

Numerous abandoned structures and shells of buildings surround the projects. They are sources for concern in the community, not only for the rats and refuse that accumulate there, but also for their use as drug-dealing locations; and they are simply depressing to see. But despite such monuments to the decline in the quality of life, old values do survive in the projects, exemplified by regular churchgoers, parents and grandparents, and other elders who believe in hard work, education, and discipline. Three representative voices of this conservatism in the black/Latino community—those of Carmen Montana, Rose Cordero, and Charles Abbott—demonstrate how vital these values are to the community, and how without them it would not exist.

Carmen Montana:
Housing Activist

The six-story buildings of the Carver project resemble more those of a project in the sleepy town of Meridian, Mississippi, than what one might expect on upper Madison Avenue in Manhattan. Narrow walkways lead from the yellow brick buildings to a flower and vegetable garden. Similar gardens can be found in the "better projects," as the tenants of these complexes call them. This garden features, among other things, tomato and pepper plants, rosebushes, and a berry patch in one corner. In back of the garden are a playground with three swings, and basketball and handball courts.

Carmen Montana, like Kimi Gray in Washington, D.C.'s Kenilworth-Parkside project and Bertha Gilkey in St. Louis's Cochran Gardens project, housing activists and charismatic, determined leaders, is an indefatigable advocate for tenants' rights and works constantly to improve public housing for residents. Tenant association president, neighborhood and project historian, and mother and grandmother, she lives on the third floor of a Carver building. In her modest apartment, where she babysits one of her grandchildren, she speaks about her family, the projects, and her life. At the building entrance downstairs, she says, are volunteer members of the tenant patrol. "We call the ledger that visitors sign in on our daily sheet. We have networks that protect tenants and young people. Of course, it's at a more informal level." There is, in addition, "a roving patrol," in which only the young men are involved. "These young people are the eyes and ears of the projects. There are a lot of other buildings, small and large, that would like to be like ours, but there is no Mrs. Montana there." She is a tough tenant leader, as she must be, to run an organization that is constantly fighting the Housing Authority bureaucracy, other tenants, gangs, and political groups. "When I became president, gangs were out. I was scared, but I wouldn't show it. I wanted them out of here, I wanted the buildings safe to be in. And with the gangs gone, nobody else like them dares come in here. You know why? Because we're going out there with help, that's why. And they know it. The people from this building and others will gather together, and somebody may get hurt physically, punched out, whatever. But drug addicts can't come in this building, I forbid it. If I see somebody that even looks like a druggie, I say, 'Who are you coming to see? Are you coming to buy drugs? Somebody selling drugs in here?' And I tell tenants: 'You can do whatever you want in your own apartment, but please, don't have people coming and going to buy drugs there. We will know in a minute. Any dirt, you do it outside. You gonna buy or sell drugs, you do it outside this project.' That's the way it is, and I tell them like it is. And they respect me for it."

Mrs. Montana relies on strategies common in many projects to involve tenants in project life. There are floor captains in the various buildings, "the eyes and ears of the buildings," many of whom volunteer for the position. There is a tenant patrol, whose members sit at building entrances and monitor comings and goings, even collecting visitors' signatures, or walk around the project to assure safety and order.

"Look at my garden fence down there, you don't see no-body hanging around that fence. They better not. Our block is nice and clean, and our buildings are family building. Public housing is good, and some people don't realize how good they have it. I get mad when I see all this vandalism and all these things. I treasure this."

Mrs. Montana, who is sixty-three, has lived in Carver for many years. She came to the United States from Puerto Rico in 1962 and lived first in Brooklyn. "When we first moved in here, we had to be screened. One parent was the breadwinner and one parent stayed home. But things weren't as bad economically as they are now. These kids, they go on and make themselves pregnant so they can have a little baby and say they need something for the baby. The baby is starving, and they're using the money to snort the coke or the crack or whatever, and that child is starving. That's why these people are on welfare. But now welfare says if you're young, you work for your money. That's good. You can't move out of the projects on welfare anymore. I can't buy a home, because one person can't accumulate that much money to put a down payment on a home. No way, not the way homes cost now. Even to get an apartment you've got to have money in the bank, so the landlord won't think you're running out at the end of the month."

In 1964, when Carver opened, New York City had nearly a million more manufacturing jobs than it does today. The Washburn Wire Company, a short distance from Carver, employed more than 450 people, many from Harlem. Other neighborhood residents commuted to jobs in other parts of the city—Queens, Brooklyn, and elsewhere on Long Island, and downtown Manhattan. Families in the projects could easily have one spouse the breadwinner, the other at home. Things are different now, as Mrs. Montana knows. "Both parents have to work to survive," so they cannot be at home for their youngsters. "Back then children weren't allowed to play in the hallways or be involved in street riots. They respected their neighbors. They respected their parents, which today you don't see. I don't mean to say you don't have good kids, because you do. This place has some very good kids. But you sometimes would like to see more of them.

"I was taught my values by my mother and father," Mrs. Montana says. "I was taught to respect my elders, whether neighbors or teachers or priests, to always have that respect. If what I was taught makes me old-fashioned, okay, then I'll be old-fashioned. As big as my kids are, I will not let them play loud music. That's the way I like to live—quiet and peaceful.

"When I grew up, kids were not supposed to talk back to their parents. Now kids are smarter. There has been a cutoff point, and the old values have not been passed on. I think a lot of single parents aren't teaching the values they were taught. When my kids were younger and their father was out working, I had to discipline them. I would tell my kids, 'When your father comes home, he's going to know about this. So there's two of us. What you did, your father is going to know, so he's going to let you have it too.' Single parents can't discipline their kids that way."

Mrs. Montana recognizes that what was discipline in the past might be termed differently today. "I know there is a lot of child abuse. When I grew up, they didn't call it that. My mother used to throw rice on the floor. 'Kneel,' she would say. And you'd kneel on those little pieces of rice for half a minute or so, and it would hurt. Blood would trickle down from those wounds. She would sometimes take a strap, wind it around her hand, and beat us." That was abusive, Mrs. Montana admits, "but you wouldn't be bad no more."

The scene outside her living room window, of teenagers on the corner slapping five and listening to the radio, prompts Mrs.

Montana: "My boys never stood on no corners. Three of them are correction officers. Their values are good. They're not bums. They're not drug addicts. They're not thieves. They haven't been in jail. Now they have their own children, their own houses. They were raised here, in this little apartment. They weren't allowed to be in that street. That was their thing, looking out the window. But they couldn't go out there. When they left here, they went to the service. At seventeen, they went. They said, 'Momma, sign this paper so I can go.' And I did."

What Montana calls old-fashioned values might be referred to as discipline. And that is what young people need to make it out of the projects and into the larger world of possibility. For this they require the implicit or explicit guidance of family—be it their real family or that constituted by after-school programs or groups such as the Writers Crew. These networks not only support young people and bring them to participate, but also make them feel accountable and responsible.

Home Training:
Values

The rules for everyday life passed down from one generation to the next might be termed "home training." These dos and don'ts, these codes of respect and manners, are more than niceties. Behind them is a value system and a great deal of discipline. That discipline applies to, among other things, striving for the best, carrying on honorably despite the odds, staying in school, taking care of family, working hard, avoiding unwanted pregnancy.

"The home is very important in the success of an adolescent," Mrs. Montana says. "It's where respect is taught. Respect for oneself, for elders." Goodness depends on the home, troublemakers are those "who lack good home learning." Parents bear a great responsibility in this respect. "When that priest tells you 'For richer, for poorer, for better, for worse,' that's what he means. If you have a family and you disagree with your husband or wife, don't think of your disagreements, think about how you will make a decision to come together. When one parent goes one way and the other parent goes the other way, there is no more respect in the house. The children like to see both parents, not just one."

Mrs. Montana hopes to pass the old values on through the generations. She tells her grandchildren to avoid anyone involved with drugs. "I don't care who they are—friends, boyfriends, girlfriends, whoever. 'Do not stay in the street hanging out,' I say. My friends used to say, 'Why you don't let them boys go out, they're bored in the house all the time. They gonna be faggots.' I said, 'If they gonna be faggots, let them be good faggots.' But they weren't faggots. They went to war. Not that faggots don't fight in wars. As a matter of fact, they probably serve a purpose there.

"I was always overprotective of my kids. I didn't want them to fight. I used to tell them, 'When you fight, it's for a good cause. You don't fight for nothing.' Some parents say, 'If somebody hit you, take a stick or a bat or something and bang their brains out.' I don't believe you should tell your kids this. You can create a monster without knowing it. We had a kid right here in Carver like that. This boy was small for his age and was always getting beat up by other kids. And people used to say, 'Get a stick, get a bat, don't let that boy hit you.' When he was fourteen, he killed a man. He didn't beat him to death, he shot him in the head in a turf war. He wanted to be a drug dealer. That kid went on to the penitentiary."

Over and over again one sees how young black males play out their rage and anger: violence against people in their own communities. The youngster Mrs. Montana has been talking about, like many in the projects today, was trapped; the larger culture restricted or closed his access to an approved way of reaching his legitimate goals or potential. Knowing nothing about the structural sources of his plight, he could not channel that rage positively.

————

Rose Cordero:
Grandmothers' Alliance

The area from 116th Street to 125th Street has been designated an economic development zone by the city. The aim is to give local business people a chance to prosper. La Marqueta, the Latino market in the area, has attracted only one major meat distributor, and other merchants who acquired space in the market complain that renovations and development they were promised have not appeared. One merchant, Nelson Ramirez, says, "I don't want to rent anymore. I want to own my own space. Why can't I do that? They don't want Latinos to make it in this city. We voted for Dinkins [in 1989], and he has not done anything for us. The Jews complain one time, and they get him running over there making concessions. This city can help us if they let us own something, instead of making us pay this rent all the time."

The city has set up the Incubator Project, which is supposed to help merchants start small enterprises in East Harlem. It is too early to tell what effect this will have on local economic development. There is talk about middle-class Latinos and blacks abandoning their poorer brethren for suburban life, but this seems to be more talked about than documented by empirical evidence. What is true is that many people leave poorer communities such as projects when they can afford to, when they are young or prosperous.

"We've had some success stories in here," Rose Cordero says about the Clinton project, where she lives. "When my brother made lots of money, he walked out of here, moved away." She mentions others who have left, but admits that "a lot of us stayed. The older ones stayed and the younger ones left. The ones that got educated and had good jobs left. But you know how we are with our folks: If Mama is there, we go back to see her.

"The neighborhood has changed, and that's the bad part. Drugs are on every corner, no matter where you walk. It's young women, it's older women, it's a woman with a baby. At what age did these girls start using drugs? Every corner you go to—you go down the block it's there, you go up the block it's there. Go out along the project benches and there is hardly any room for our older citizens to sit. If it's not an addict sitting there, it's a homeless person."

Mrs. Cordero describes how she moved from anonymous citizen to community leader. "When I first attended tenant meetings, the lady running them didn't have a secretary. Since I spoke both English and Spanish she asked me would I take the minutes. Then, when her time in the position was up, I was elected president. As president I deal with everything—from maintenance to security problems, the whole thing. We try to make management more accessible to us. But we don't have that much power. Sometimes I feel I have input into the decision-making process, and sometimes I don't. What we do have is power to choose. For example, tenants are going to get new cabinets and sinks. The tenant association will be involved. We will go and look at them and approve some."

Clinton's active tenant group is run mostly by women, and Mrs. Cordero likens the community to a big family with women playing the dominant role. "The women are there," she says, "because the men see this as women's work. But men participate too. I try to have Saturday as our meeting day, because everybody is home on Saturday. As president, I'm very straightforward. I tell you what I gotta tell you. You either tell me yes or no. You don't dilly-dally with me."

Mrs. Cordero's attitude reflects her traditional family background. "There was Mom and Pop. My father worked. My mother was home with us. She took us to school, the doctor, whatever. We came from Puerto Rico, and in those days if you were to come up pregnant it was a tragedy. Today, when any young lady comes up pregnant she has a choice of abortion or keeping it and going on welfare. Only in rare circumstances does the young man marry her and go to work and support her. Young ladies and young men of today missed out on their families. We had a grandma who would tell us about the past. Well, the grandma of today is out there selling or using crack. Kids today are missing out on a lot because they have no more values."

Many people, however, would point to the key role grandmothers play in maintaining stability among project families. They would also insist that kids do get values, if sometimes from outside the home; when these outside values conflict with those from inside the home, the differences must be reconciled.

Mrs. Cordero holds fast to certain ideals and has tried to pass them on to her children. "I've put into their head since they were little what's right and what's wrong. Once my kids leave the house, they know how to behave. Whoever tells them whatever in the street, it's up to them to decide. I hope, of course, that they will decide to do what I taught them, not what is out there in the street."

Most parents today are not as strict as she was, Mrs. Cordero says, and "they just don't have time to be with their kids. I feel very sad for kids who don't have that unity of family. Most of what is considered family in the projects are single-parent arrangements. And most are headed by women."

Exactly what does constitute a family has become controversial recently, in New York City and across the country. Many people see the family as any unit in which the basic necessities of food, shelter, and clothing, and love, attention, and values are afforded its members. Project residents object to the idea that a single parent and the children he or she is bringing up do not constitute a family. Single parenthood, it must be pointed out, is a fact of life not only in the projects. According to Census Bureau data for 1990 on households with young children, the number in which a married couple headed the family was 26 percent of the total—down from 40 percent in 1970. These ever-larger numbers of single-parent families in the United States would once have been termed "broken families." Yet these and other family configurations are not necessarily good or bad. Instead, as reflections of the changing shape of the American family over the last quarter-century, they are signs of a dynamic rather than a static society.

Mrs. Cordero reiterates the importance of values, whatever the individual family arrangement. With boys and girls socialized differently, are they also taught different sets of values? As a rule, it seems, society favors boys and men. Boys can "hang out," while girls are "locked up" or must be home by a certain hour. Boys are more often "pushed out" of the house at the end of adolescence, whereas girls are kept at home until they find a suitable boy to marry. Mrs. Cordero, who has only daughters, maintains that she would have brought up sons exactly as she did her daughters. "They would have had the same values. Any boy of mine would have had curfews."

Skepticism seems to be Mrs. Cordero's attitude toward many values today's young people pick up from outside the family. "When I was growing up we didn't have a TV. We had to read the newspaper or magazines or comic books or listen to the radio. Today they have everything. And oh, God, this TV stuff is turning out to be very bad." She mentions popular music as another source of values that do not coincide with her own. Although she doesn't normally listen to "that rap stuff," she remembers lyrics in which "a girl is saying that she liked her girlfriend's boyfriend and she's going to take him away from her. That's not what I taught my daughters. I taught my daughters to have respect for what belongs to somebody else. If a girl is going out with a guy and you like him, you leave it alone, because he belongs to her. You have to be in that girl's place. How would you feel if someone came along and take your guy away? I give my daughters a lesson, and here comes the rap music telling them it's okay to do something bad." Even if such lyrics are not meant to be taken literally or seriously, Mrs. Cordero is adamant that they can have a negative influence on young people. As just one example she cites girls' learning how to curse. "Listen to them—curse, curse, curse, just like they were boys. You walk down the street and hear, 'Oh, you get f——' and 'Get the f—— away from me.' I have had to debrief my kids in the after-school program. They know better than to speak any profane or insulting language when they come here."

Mrs. Cordero's after-school program is more than just a place for kids to while away time. Here, as in some other "safe places," norms about desirable behavior are established for these kids, and reinforced in them. And Mrs. Cordero is more than just a monitor. She is an adult whom young people seek to emulate and from whom they receive implicit and explicit messages on how to comport themselves. She is, in effect, part of their extended family.

Stability and
Family Buildings

Carmen Montana refers to "family buildings," those in which residents are as concerned about one another as they would be about blood relatives. She remembers that these used to be the rule rather than the exception. Everyone "could feel comfortable. It wasn't as bad as it is now. But now with this crack epidemic, it's become hard. Things are messed up. People won't come out of their houses like they used to." Her own building is a family building. "We watch each other. Nobody hurts nobody here. And it's only six stories: we know who's who, who lives here and who doesn't. We have people who care. Anybody who comes in and doesn't live here, I'm going to find out why that person came in." In a tall building, Mrs. Montana says, tenants can't keep track.

Certainly it is not simply the height of a building, but also what type of people live in it and whether they support one another, that determines its safety and security. Yet at least one study of New York City projects, which showed that the number of robberies in buildings was directly proportional to height, suggests that high-rise designs contribute to rising crime rates. High-rise buildings, it should be pointed out, are built to save on land and land costs. Across the United States, high-rises account for 27 percent of public housing buildings; most of them are located in large urban centers. Garden apartments constitute 32 percent, low-rise walk-ups 16 percent, and single-family houses or townhouses 25 percent.

▬▬▬▬

Parents and Safety

Parents in the projects rely on various strategies to steer their children away from danger and to make safety zones for them. To create these desirable niches for their children outside the schools, parents join together in tenant associations, coordinate their efforts with those of project managers, and reach out to such institutions as churches and social welfare agencies. They often assume responsibility for surveillance in project public spaces and common rooms, and individually they involve their children in after-school activities meant to ensure their safety and positive growth, and enlist the help of professionals in community agencies. The success of youngsters in public housing projects seems directly related to how well parents and their allies are able to provide safe niches for them. The relationship is difficult to prove empirically, however, in part because the projects exist within a constellation of neighborhoods, which means youngsters may face unpredictable risks from outside the project where they live. Every project may constitute a neighborhood, but it is also only part of a neighborhood composed of other projects and nonproject buildings.

Many residents of East Harlem, particularly along Madison Avenue, do not feel safe; they would like more lighting in public places, and would rather see new housing or parks or other amenities than vacant lots. Nurses, doctors, and other employees of Mount Sinai Hospital, the largest institution in the area, likewise do not feel safe. They have supported the efforts of Civitas, a community organization to assess the needs of the community. A survey conducted among 800 residents in five housing projects (among the interviewers were members of the Writers Crew) found that many were less concerned about crime than about teenage pregnancy and the lack of activities for young people.

The manager of the J. W. Johnson project, Mrs. Thompson, is a tall, dark woman, businesslike but charming and pleasant to talk to. Terry Williams meets her in her office, which is more orderly and spacious than other Harlem project offices, and better equipped, with three computers and a large printer. She grew up in a Brooklyn project, and one of her two sisters, who made it out of the projects, is also a project manager. She offers statistics on the racial makeup of "her project"—55 percent Latino, 45 percent black—and says there are no real racial tensions.

"Mrs. Cordero believes that the projects should be co-managed by tenants and 250 Broadway [the address of the City Housing Authority headquarters]," she says smiling. "But if that happens, I'll be out of work. One of the things we are sticklers for, though, is tenant selection. We want families and some individuals. We favor families over single persons, except in the case of the homeless. The homeless preempt everyone, because they pass over the waiting list. The elderly and disabled also have a great priority position. And the families must be low-income. People may wait several years before they get an apartment here. Because of the loss of spaces to the incoming homeless, we have turned a blind eye to doubling up." Consequently, while the New York City Housing Authority may define "family" for apartments in its control as two or more persons living together as a cohesive group, the reality is often looser and broader.

The extent and meaning of "family," then, have necessarily changed, not only so people can find a place to live in one project or another, but also as they struggle with single parenting, teenage pregnancy, and a loss of job opportunities for young people. Mothers are left to bring up their children alone, as fathers are absent from the home, and grandmothers play an ever larger role. Mrs. Thompson, who was brought up by her mother, nonetheless remembers the influence her grandmother held over her mother. "My mother always told us that education was the priority for guaranteeing a safe future. She said her mother taught her that and she was teaching us the same way. She said without her mother's wisdoms, she would have strayed long before my sisters and I were born."

It is a quick walk from the Johnson project to Carver. Although statistics suggest that Carver, with its low crime rate and better record of children's school enrollment, is a more desirable place to live, on this day it seems dirty and neglected compared with Johnson. The grass at Carver is high, the courtyard littered with trash. A few people are in the playground—four older men on a bench eating lunch, and a girl on a swing. She asks for the time as Terry and Mrs. Thompson pass by. Near the Carver management office, a young man sitting alone on a bench smiles somewhat anxiously in their direction. He looks as if he is dreaming, and motions for them to come over. He wears neat, pleated pants and a checkered sports jacket; his face is distorted, and his eyes are lost within themselves. He looks up and asks, "Where can I get some water around here?" then folds his hands into his lap. He is obviously high, and suffering through a difficult time of it.

Meanwhile, from elsewhere in the neighborhood come the voices of students from Central Park East Secondary School, which is letting out now. Central Park East is one of the most innovative alternative schools run by the New York City Board of Education. Near the school is the Graffiti Hall of Fame, decorated by local and other graffiti artists; this attracts the attention of many of the students.

Terry and Mrs. Thompson move quickly to the Carver office, which though small is brightly painted and filled with sunshine. Antidrug messages cover a bulletin board, one of them a "warning to drug dealers": "Stay the hell out of public housing." Who knows how many drug dealers have been frightened by, or even seen, this sign.

The assistant manager of Carver, Marie Della, who is white and lives on Staten Island, seems out of place here. She admits that she is new to the community and explains further: "I was given a promotion. I wanted to stay in Staten Island, but I didn't want to stay in a low position. So when I got the chance to be promoted, I had to go where the promotion was. And this is it."

Calm, intelligent, well spoken, Ms. Della sees the community as a "good place, with good people." She mentions the work records of people who have been at Carver longer than she, and she expresses respect for the tenants, who do well managing themselves. "Carmen Montana, our historian around here, is an excellent tenant association president."

A thirty-year-old architectural plan for Carver hangs on one wall of the office. It shows four high-rise and six low-rise buildings. Ms. Della considers the low-rise superior to the high-rise, "because there is a better community atmosphere. The low-rises are less impersonal. They foster neighborliness."

Charles Abbott:
Housing Bureaucrat

Charles Abbott is the voice of ultraconservatism in the black community. He represents those who are angry with the way the race has "degenerated" and who look forward to a day when the family is male-dominated, women have their "place," and children speak only when spoken to. The newly minted manager of one of the larger projects—thirteen buildings—he knows his way around and freely expresses his opinions.

Mr. Abbott, who looks to be in his forties, is a short, thin, light-complexioned black man. He chain-smokes and gestures nervously; his handshake is strong. He strikes one as a person fond of bureaucracy, and a conversation with him soon turns into a monologue on his part.

"We have more data on computer disk on each of our tenants than the federal government has on Americans," he says proudly. He patches together a quilt of public policy language, bureaucratese, and social science references. "We have many disadvantaged families, but the images of poverty are not at all what Oscar Lewis calls a culture."

Mr. Abbott harps against the media for their portrayal of public housing. Most members of the media, he maintains, are "hateful people who detest public housing. All their little petty prejudices surface when they do stories about us." Yet Mr. Abbott admits to disliking both Carver and Harlem. "Most of these people don't care about themselves or their families. They don't work to keep their places up, and don't work much at all."

The computerized record-keeping system holds his interest, however, and he continues proudly: "We'll make compiling statistics really painless, so that almost everything can be asked of the tenants and they must comply with our requests. PIMS, the Project Information Management System, records family composition, income, ethnicity, race, nationality—you name it. Much of the family data is changing as the definition of family is opened.

"BAMS, the Bookkeeping Automated Management System, records the income of those on public assistance" and tells "when their payments are due, if they've been paid, and the like." This is to keep track of rent payments as well, since rent is paid out of assistance income. In times of need, says Mr. Abbott, some tenants use their rent allotment for other expenses. When the New York City Housing Authority loses 10 percent of its rent in a particular project, it may cut aid to that project. Managers are thus eager to have their tenants pay rent on time. BAMS "allows managers to get to that assistance money first, before it goes to some other expense." Mr. Abbott points out that all NYCHA project rents for similar apartments are the same, if the project budgets are the same, and that 85 percent of the budget is federally funded, 10 percent state funded, and 5 percent city funded.

When asked about families leaving the projects, Mr. Abbott goes on at length. "Many families use the projects as a stepping-stone into the middle class, buying co-ops, homes, you know. We have a program called Project Home, which places families who have incomes higher than the range required for living in the projects. The program allows these families to save for homes in the private sector, mostly in Queens. Families are chosen for their good standing, and their honest and regular reporting of income to management. As yet, there are no credit checks, although proposals have been made to run checks. Most data on families comes from their project history."

Mr. Abbott notes that New York City has the best-run public housing in the country, "because of three things: tenant patrols, community involvement, volunteer services." But there are problems within project families, mainly problems related to children—"and all is largely due to the absence of male figures in the home. Many single-parent households have problems with discipline, and once the mother goes wrong, the children are bound to go wrong too. Male figures are central to the move into private homes. Single-parent families rarely move out, because the economics are against them."

Mr. Abbott implies that female heads of households are not strong role models, and in fact are the major cause of problems in families. "Most of these women can't teach economics successfully. They can't be the best role models for boys, because the boys don't respect them as parents. Their parenting skills are poor. Households degenerate because they don't have a strong male authority."

One other major problem in the projects involves what Mr. Abbott calls the "worst cases"—the formerly homeless who are newly admitted into public housing. "They may be former tenants, some evicted for causing trouble, but they are now let in again because of a mayoral decree." Some people believe this decree was the city's way of forcing the working poor out of public housing. Mayor Edward Koch's administration gave many homeless families priority in entering the projects, and some tenant leaders resented this measure as an attack on poor blacks and Latinos. But not all project residents or managers view the homeless negatively. Mrs. Johnson at Martin Luther King Towers, for instance, sees them as people in need, like other tenants at one time or another. The only chance other tenants may have to prevent such admissions is to be part of the screening process for applicants. The screening council includes the manager, the tenant association president (who, Mr. Abbott says, "is the one with the real power. They can make me disappear in a minute"), and the tenant association committee.

Drugs too constitute a problem at Carver. "A lot of homeless people, drug users or sellers, have come into our buildings," says Mr. Abbott. "They bring garbage from the dumpsters to sleep on, they defecate, they urinate in halls and stairwells. They eat there. They leave their trash and body waste behind. The projects were supposed to be a stepping-stone for the common people. Given a chance, they were supposed to move into homes eventually. But for most of them it didn't turn out that way. The projects become home."

Abbott says migrating out of Harlem proper, into middle-class or working-class neighborhoods in Brooklyn and Queens, is what most of the families in the projects should be doing. "Ethnically mixed neighborhoods are more stable," he argues. But "when Co-op City in the Bronx opened up to blacks and Latinos, whites immediately left."

Mr. Abbott himself grew up in a private home in the Williamsburg section of Brooklyn. He says his greatest advantage was having been reared in this ethnically mixed neighborhood, and he is an advocate for preserving such neighborhoods: "If a community is integrated, it should stay integrated. Because once people leave, they don't come back. And once you leave people behind, they become socially isolated. When residents do well, they should return to give encouragement." Recent sociological findings suggest that too often the opposite happens. As William Wilson has noted in his book *The Truly Disadvantaged,* among the reasons for new poverty in communities are "the outmigration of nonpoor black families" and "the exodus of white and other nonblack families," as well as heavy job losses.

Mr. Abbott talks about various ongoing activities within Carver. While there are no on-site child-care centers, there is a social network to steer kids into safe places. And the Housing Authority sponsors programs for tenants. "We have a talent search program called Carver Day and area community centers like Casita Maria. And I put together this newsletter for tenants to read and enjoy. But you know, even with the bright color [it's printed on bright yellow paper], most tenants don't pick it up." When he once asked a tenant why she didn't pick up a copy, she told him to "forget the yellow, I want the green"—money.

Carver's manager, as has been seen, does not hide his complaints about tenants. Most of them, he says, "rarely make use of the bulletin board, and there are many notices about scholarships, jobs for kids, and the like. They just don't care. Sometimes I think we have a problem of information overload.

"Problem tenants know how to use the system, for instance the landlord-tenant court. They know how to prolong the time in which they can go without paying rent. They drag out the drama for up to two years and then leave when the decision is handed down." All of this "legal mumbo-jumbo," Mr. Abbott says, prevents project staff from working on efforts that would benefit the larger community. When tenants engage in dilatory or evasive tactics, they set examples: "The kids emulate them, and end up doing the same things when they get an apartment." The legal entanglements often become a game of "Let's Make a Deal" when the Housing Authority tries to avoid what Mr. Abbott calls "risk situations." "When you evict people, it causes bad PR all around. Take, for example, evicting a family with kids, or old people, or people who are sick or disabled. That's bad PR. I remember I had a guy with crutches who used to openly deal drugs in here. I tried to get him evicted, and this guy had all the media down here. It was a real media event, and all hell broke loose about the NYCHA evicting a disabled man."

The spring weather is breaking here at Carver, and Terry Williams sits on a bench in a quiet part of the project, reflecting on managers and tenants alike. He is temporarily distracted by two teenage maintenance workers in blue NYCHA uniforms as they pick up debris from the grounds. A woman walking with her two-year-old grandson stops to talk with Terry. She tells him about the playground. The equipment is new, and concrete has been replaced with soft rubber padding. One can only imagine the struggle between the Housing Authority and the tenant association over funding for this safer setup. The neighborhood shows other signs of struggle: there are stark abandoned buildings here and there, and crack vials on the steps of many a building. Battles are still being fought, and it is unclear whether there will be any winners. And yet this area—indeed, Harlem in general—is primed for a renaissance, both cultural and structural. Real estate speculation abounds; buildings are considered for landmarking; an air of stability in the projects and out keeps the community from disintegrating entirely. The projects are an oasis in a troubled neighborhood.

Prime Property

"Manhattan is prime property," Carmen Montana says, and to her that means that housing projects are prime property too. "All sorts of people want to come up here, move in here." She wants to organize a Carver Day, for people in all thirteen buildings to get together in a community celebration. Mrs. Montana comments on Carver's manager: "Mr. Abbott, he's so nice, a wonderful person. He's backing us up one hundred percent." And she praises the staff—"the best by far. Everything is coming together good."

Indeed, everything is coming together well, just as the world is coming to Harlem for its young people, its ideas, and its culture. The community is producing culture and excitement within and beyond its borders. Perhaps it is not yet another Harlem renaissance, but there is movement in that direction. There are new cottage industries and other small business enterprises, and an increasing emphasis on intellectual capital, leisure, and services.

And threaded through this resurgence is an ongoing ethnic mix: the community includes the new Peruvian eatery as well as the old Cuban restaurant, the more recently arrived Nigerian hair-braider and the longtime resident African-American barber. All of this despite racism—or perhaps as a response to it: many might see this cultural renewal in part as a reaction to a history of oppression. In effect, though, it is a reaction to and balance for such negative elements in the community as violence and drugs.

Dexter
(Photograph by Brian Kennedy)

CHAPTER 8

Growing Up

"I got things on my mind," Jack tells Terry Williams. "My attitude is up in arms right now." They are at a Village club awaiting a jazz/hip-hop performance by a friend of Jack's. "I'm still homeless. But I don't understand why. The type of person I am, all the people I know, all the places I've been, all the wonderful things I've done and want to do in my life—I never thought in a hundred years I would be in this situation."

The "situation" is on his mind all night. "I'm not going to let myself get into this type of situation again once I get back on my feet," he says an hour later over loud music. "I know I need help, but for some reason I feel like I can't ask anyone to help me. I need a better job so I can save some money and find an apartment or a room somewhere. I had started to make preparations for a trip out to San Francisco because I wanted to get a job with a friend of my uncle's at a radio station out there. But I want to be on my own so I won't have to ask anybody for nothing."

Terry drives Jack home after the show, and Jack insists Terry see how he is living.

"I thought you said you were homeless," Terry says as Jack directs him to park in front of a five-story brownstone."

"Just wait a minute," Jack responds. "I have been living from friend to friend for six months as I told you, and that's why I haven't been to Writers Crew meetings. I told my uncle about my situation, and he says I could stay with him if I did a little work around the house. The house turn out to be kinda like a crack house and the work is kinda like being a bouncer." Having been turned out by his mother after constant conflicts, Jack has decided to stay with his uncle. His uncle's place is indeed a crack house and he is the house bouncer, albeit part-time. He has taken a room on the top floor.

He leads Terry through a rusty, creaking iron gate and into the kitchen area. Cupboards are open cabinets and reveal assorted pots and pans. A table in the center is stacked with dishes. Water flows from the faucet into the sink. On the opposite side of the room stands a padlocked refrigerator. "Only my uncle has the key to that lock," Jack says, as he goes on to a small, dark room. Here there is a wooden table crowded by worn and broken chairs; missing arms and legs of the chairs lie in the crowded corners. From the walls and ceiling hang remnants of musical instruments: a hollow bass fiddle, a keyless saxophone, a flute missing its bottom, a stringless guitar, an oboe with chopsticks protruding from it, a rusting clarinet emerging from a burst drum.

Despite the hour—it is three-thirty in the morning—the doorbell rings. "There are people upstairs, I'm sure," Jack says, "and more will be coming in here all night long." Jack goes to the gate and immediately gets into an argument with the couple there. They refuse to pay the obligatory fee of crack or money to the owner of the house, and Jack accordingly refuses them entry. He's had previous run-ins with the man. Finally the couple gives up, the man saying he'll come back later. "This is what I have to contend with," Jack says with disgust. "Everybody knows you gotta pay a pc [a small gratuity] to Big Bob to get in here. I knocked this one dude in the head with a billy club because he was acting all fucked up around here. As the bouncer, I have the right to do this. I lit into that motherfucker. I hit him and his head swelled up as big as a grapefruit. I'll only be here another two weeks, though. Another two weeks, and my life will be better. This is crazy, and the people here are crazy. I've got to get out."

Three weeks later Jack leaves the crack house and moves in with his girlfriend in an apartment in the Bronx. One wonders how long he can stay there, without a job and with an attitude reflecting his struggle to find himself. And he has big news: He is father to a seven-pound baby girl. "I want to be the best father I can to my baby," he says. Yet Terry Williams sees little effort on Jack's part to change his circumstances. He appears hell-bent on self-destructive behavior and needs more help than the Writers Crew, for one, can give him now.

Being a Parent

Sheena, for her part, is trying to reconcile her relationship with her grandmother as she strives to be a good mother to her daughter. Her grandmother moved, and Sheena had to find her own place. Sheena's brother too has been having problems. His came to a head when his grandmother refused to take him in as a probationary condition after he was arrested.

"We had to do this custody thing in the courtroom," explains Sheena. "They had a lawyer for grandmother, but Billy was not represented. If my grandmother didn't agree to take him, he would have to go to jail. They said they would place him with my grandmother for ninety days, but she said no, she would only take him for two weeks.

"That night my grandmother just flipped on me. She told me to take all my stuff and get out, and take the baby's things too. The court says my brother has to go to counseling, and we would probably have to go too, but my grandmother is seventy years old and she's tired of all of this. I understand. So I told the court I would take Billy temporarily, because my grandmother agreed to help me get an apartment."

Sheena had barely gotten her things settled into the new place when her brother appeared at the door, bleeding and scared. "I just looked at him. I was so disgusted. I tried to be calm. I asked him what happened and he said somebody beat him up because he owes them money. He was selling crack for this dealer, and when they came to get their money he said somebody robbed him. They didn't believe him, beat him up, knocked a tooth out, and he's fucked up. They want their money back. He just got to grow up and learn to keep his ass out of the projects. It's not my beef, so I didn't feel like I should be getting the money back for him."

Sheena realized then that she was a parent not only to her baby but to her brother as well. "He sat there crying and shaking, and I tried to think of ways to get the money." She never got the money, and her brother continued avoiding the dealers to whom he owed money. "They told him he had to work off the debt." Since then Billy was arrested for violating parole, and he sat in a Manhattan detention center facing two to five years in jail. Sheena cried when she heard about it. "I tried as hard as I could to help him," she says, "but he was hardheaded and wanted to make that money and live large, and he was never all of that. He got in with the wrong company, never been out of trouble since he was fourteen."

Sheena took on more responsibility regarding her brother.

She wrote him letters, visited him in jail, and sent him commissary money when she could. Her grandmother didn't feel obligated to do so once he violated probation, and after several months Sheena fell off in her visiting and had little money to send. She is saddened by the whole affair and wishes she could do more. "But I got my baby to take care of, and myself too. I got so many problems now that I don't know what to do. I try to laugh, but nothing but tears come out."

Giant Steps

Dexter, on probation and at risk for dropping out of school again, was able to find some odd jobs. At the City University Graduate Center, where Terry Williams and Bill Kornblum arranged for some temporary employment, he even spent time learning to write on the computer. People who have been intimidated by writing in school often get a big lift from mastering a computer keyboard. They forget their fear and hesitations. For Dexter the problem was not the act of writing itself—he has always been highly creative and insightful—but command of various voices and functions: the formal voice of a business letter, the informed voice of an essay or newsletter article, and so on. The computer, of course, made the task of editing much easier for him, and within weeks he was making great leaps forward.

All this went on during the spring, when nearby Bryant Park and girls in lighter street clothes beckoned. It was not the best time for a young man to connect with schoolwork. Despite the distractions, however, Dexter devoted himself to his studies. He worked at math, and his writing output increased dramatically. Terry and Bill encouraged him and helped him with questions and problems. But Dexter himself seemed to have decided that he could study and get his GED, and thereby participate even more in the life of learning.

"I need to get this GED and get the hell out of the Annex," he repeated during those months. "You know how that school is? It's like some of the teachers are okay, but almost everyone there is into styling and profiling and hustles. You see more fat jewelry than in a jeweler's shop. This girl there told me she was only going to be there for a week. Then she was going back to her regular high school. She was on suspension. See, they send kids there for punishment."

The space, the quiet, and the support he found at the Graduate Center gave Dexter a needed boost. He took the GED test but failed it. He did not give up, however—this was a positive sign—and resolved to take it again. The next month he did, and he passed.

When he received the news, Dexter radiated a quiet glow of satisfaction that had never been seen before. Everyone at the Graduate Center who had come to know him was overjoyed when he shyly told them he had gotten his degree. Here was someone who had been labeled an educational failure, achieving an intellectual breakthrough. If he had successfully defended a doctoral dissertation there would not have been more congratulations and invitations to celebrate. Dexter himself, the stigma and the burden of the barriers it represented lifted from his young shoulders, seemed to have grown taller overnight.

Where the Buffalo Roam

The spring and summer continued to be rewarding for Dexter. Terry and Bill were organizing a test survey of visitors to national parks for the National Park Service and needed interviewers. The project would test a methodology and questionnaire that eventually would be used to monitor growing public use of national parks. Six interviewers and two supervisors would spend a week or so in eight major national parks. They would begin in the East and the South, then return briefly to New York, and continue the survey in the West. Interviews would be conducted with more than fifteen hundred visitors chosen at random in the most popular recreation areas.

Dexter, along with Paco, was ready and willing. They had both worked on surveys before, including one about Manhattan's Central Park. Both had proven themselves to be talented interviewers in public places. Yet neither had ever visited a national park. To camp out under the stars was beyond their wildest imagination.

Paco sounded more confident than Dexter about the upcoming trip: "I will be visiting places I've never been before, all natural areas with camping and that sort of thing, places that aren't overly commercialized." After the trip, even though he regretted not being able to do any artwork, Paco said he enjoyed camping, and the feeling of being "so small in the universe. You get a chance to get into your own head. To see the mountains and the rivers and all that was very fulfilling."

Dexter was having a hard time conceiving of getting out of Harlem. Neither had much of an idea what would be involved in such a research assignment. They would soon embark on a series of adventures and hard work that would open their eyes to the nation beyond Manhattan. "I want to get out of Manhattan, but I don't know what to expect. This will be a learning experience, camping in another part of the world. Because that part of the country is like another world for me."

The last few days before the trip were hectic. There were hours of training for the team to complete, and details regarding packing, supplies, arrangements with National Park Service managers, and so on had to be attended to. All the interviewers needed travel and salary advances to cover expenses. It seemed, finally, that all was in order. But fifteen minutes before the bank closed on the Friday they were to leave, Bill Kornblum got a frantic call from Dexter and Paco at the nearby bank. For unexplained reasons the bank would not cash their checks without a letter from their supervisor. The other interviewers, who had their own bank accounts, were having no such problems. Dexter and Paco, their picture ID cards from CUNY in hand, wondered whether the problem had anything to do with their being African-American kids from uptown. They had no bank accounts, no credit cards. There was no time for Bill to get over to the bank with the letter. Dexter and Paco eventually had to pay to have their checks cashed in a check-cashing store. This small but intensely frustrating incident was the harbinger of many similar ones throughout the summer.

The first park the team visited was a cinch. In Prince William Forest, an old conservation camp now used for group outings from Washington, D.C., and Baltimore especially, interviews had gone well despite some rain. The next park was Assateague Island National Seashore in Maryland and Virginia, one of the major barrier island seashore parks on the East Coast. Here the team would try to camp in the park and do interviewing during the day. This turned into a minor disaster. Only two of the interviewers had any camping experience. The others had claimed that sleeping bags and tents would be no problem for them, but the reality proved otherwise. After the first day of work at Assateague, the team set about clumsily pitching tents in the ample campground. It was pitch-dark before they crawled, exhausted, into the unfamiliar shelter. A cold wind whipped sand around them all night. Dexter and Paco shivered in their sleeping bags and worried about every noise they heard from outside the flapping tent. They awoke the next morning stiff and miserable, each vowing never to go camping again. Some of the others were equally miserable, but they were hesitant about complaining too much: they had agreed before that camping in the parks should be part of the experience, as it would provide useful information.

Dexter and Paco were on the phone to Terry and Bill early that morning. Camping, they said, would not do; it was too much; it was awful. This problem was not unexpected, and enough money had been budgeted to accommodate in nearby motels those who could not camp comfortably. It was agreed that participants who felt camping interfered with their work could sleep in inexpensive motels, at least for the first half of the survey. Later in the journey, Dexter and Paco tried camping again, and met with more success, but they were never fully comfortable. A year after the trip Dexter reflected: "I never stopped to think what I was going through. A lot of what I went through was culture shock. I had to deal with white people like I never had to before. But basically it was just do what you have to do and move to the next location. I was growing up."

A few days before he was scheduled to leave the city for the park trip, Dexter had been invited to speak at his graduation from the Annex. His teachers were impressed with the way in which he had caught on to school. They knew he was beginning to speak publicly and write about his experiences. He was impressed with the invitation but reluctant to miss any of the trip. Arrangements were made so that he could fly to New York for the graduation ceremony. This was Dexter's first airplane flight, and he stayed in the city two days, long enough to appear at his graduation. He then rejoined the research team at Great Smoky Mountains National Park in Tennessee.

The summer passed in a rush of varied experiences and exhausting work. Dexter and Paco were discouraged at how few minority visitors there were in the parks. And early on they seemed somewhat blasé about the travel. The country was all too vast and different, and the towns they saw were slow compared to the city they were used to. Gradually, however, the immensity and diverse beauty began to affect them deeply. Although he was homesick for his friends and neighborhood, Dexter expressed his awe at what he was seeing.

One night at an almost empty diner near Badlands National

Park in South Dakota, Dexter started talking to a Sioux waitress and teasing her a bit in the Harlem manner. On a trip back to the kitchen she mentioned to her manager that a strange young man was speaking to her. The manager immediately assumed that Dexter was hassling her, and he sought out Dexter's supervisor to complain. He complained about Dexter also to National Park Service authorities. Terry Williams and Bill Kornblum, in New York, received a phone call from an officious South Dakota park ranger who felt he needed to inform them about the "situation." Of course there was no "situation." Whatever there had been was a simple case of misunderstanding. Dexter felt more uneasy than he had before. He had wanted to speak with Native Americans, and he did not believe he had scared the waitress; rather, the white supervisor had immediately assumed here was a black man making trouble.

The Badlands themselves may disturb city people who have never encountered the geologic indifference of nature. The jagged, inhospitable terrain may induce strange moods. With this force of nature, and the racial incident or whatever it was, Dexter's loneliness and homesickness intensified. He later remembered feeling "strange being out there. I didn't know quite how to handle that. But I was all right after talking a little bit." Fortunately, he reached out to Bill Kornblum's psychologist wife, Susan. She spent some time on the phone with him and helped him interpret and master his feelings.

In Wyoming, at Grand Teton and Yellowstone, Dexter and Paco enjoyed full exposure to two crown jewels among the national parks. They saw Old Faithful and waded in icy lakes, and met with somewhat greater success than on the East Coast when they tried camping again. On their day off from interviewing they went rafting on the Snake River.

An overnight stay in Las Vegas proved none too happy, for Dexter at least. He was thrown into a funk, perhaps because of the abrupt passage from the splendor of the Wyoming landscape to the frenzied grasping of the casinos. He saw again how few blacks there were among the tourists, and seemed to meet nasty, racially suspicious people wherever he turned. Again he felt homesick.

His mood changed again in Utah's Bryce Canyon, where the team was lodged in a modest but spacious cabin. To his great surprise, Dexter met a young white woman from out West who took an interest in him, and with whom he talked and laughed as if they had known each other for years. He was stunned; never had he imagined he could feel comfortable with a woman so different from himself. She knew nothing about New York or about his kind of life, and she was not interested in money or jewelry or clothes. Dexter did not feel embarrassed with her, for if she had had more formal education, he had had more, or at least different, experiences with life and death. The two of them talked for hours on end every day when Dexter's work was done, and sometimes even during his work. The bond between them made it hard when Dexter had to move on from Bryce Canyon to Mesa Verde National Park in Colorado. But the ability to share his feelings with someone else, with no reminder of a racial gulf, buoyed Dexter's spirits.

Mesa Verde, with its world-famous Indian cave dwellings, was the last park the research team visited. Dexter and Paco had not known of this place before, and they felt directly the deficiency of an education that failed to teach about the land's non-European inhabitants. They wanted to learn more about the ruins and the ancient culture they belonged to, but time—and their own desire to return home—would not allow it.

Dexter and Paco were in a hurry to get back to Harlem, but once there they longed to voyage again. Their heads were full of the grandeur of the West. They swelled with pride to know that in their own way they had conquered the continent and could return in the future. As Dexter told Terry Williams, "This was the best experience of my life. It was great, man, great."

In the next weeks Dexter and Paco talked about their trip at Writers Crew meetings. The other Crew members, who enjoyed hearing about the beauty of places they had never been, were themselves moving beyond established confines. The world was opening up for all of them.

Prospective Professor Marcus

At one of the Writers Crew sessions, Marcus delineates a profile not unlike his own, and describes a path some like him have followed. His strong words reflect his struggle with difficult questions of intellectual and social growth as he moves along his own path toward a professional life.

"A young black man, born in the 'ghetto' of any large city. Strong fellow, good-looking, good-natured, articulate. But poor. He has learned the value of hard work from his extended family. He has always done well in school; and now he attends a prestigious university. Here he begins his training to be a player in corporate America. He is popular in college and has friends who are black, white, everything else. His popularity protects him from blatant racism. He knows there are severe hardships in black communities, and that racism is in great part to blame. But he knows some 'good white people,' and thus theorizes that 'all that radical Black Student Union shit' cannot be quite correct.

"For this kind of black man," Marcus continues, "the bottom line is that each individual is responsible for himself and his condition. Therefore his goals are based on individualism and personal gain. A career at IBM is not far off, and investments in profitable stocks and a house in the suburbs—what he feels is a good neighborhood—soon follow. His bourgeois attitude makes it easy to sever his ties with his old community, especially 'all them lazy niggers' he grew up with. As a black man with money he is recognized as a success, but I submit he is one of the black community's greatest failures. He is dependent on whites for his salary, for his life-style, for his identity. The middle-class he belongs to is a creation of the white man.

"The 'bougie' brother has no political power because he is politically naive. A registered Democrat, he's been waiting on Tip O'Neill and Ted Kennedy and Jimmy Carter and on and on. He has no economic power because even if he got together with all the other bougie boys, Mobil Oil could buy them out tomorrow. He loves Mozart as much as Miles, Browning as much as Baraka, and Greece more, much more, than Ghana. He is Eurocentric. He has been neutralized by the white community. He has become alienated from his own. In college he learned a new language—white-boy English. He has forgotten ebonics. His children are named John and Susie and will be raised as Episcopalians. This is no success. This is the transformation of the African."

Marcus pauses and looks around at the other members of the Writers Crew. "I could give more details on bougie boys, but most of us know at least one. The wild shit is that I could have easily wound up like that. White folks have plans for black men, and my life has come in contact with these plans. We gotta remember that there is more than one plan. Racism ain't easy no more. It's what they call dynamic. The shit changes on you: One minute this way, the next minute that way. One minute the door is closed, the next minute it's open—but you can't get in. The next minute you're in, but you're stuck in the corner. The next minute you're at the table, but you can't speak. The next minute you can speak, but no one is listening. One minute you're a slave, the next minute you're not. The more things change, the more they stay the same."

Escape Routes:
Fits and Starts

The kids in the Writers Crew each have their own paths to follow, paths that are neither simple nor predictable. Albeit with fits and starts, they are becoming adults and taking on the responsibilities adulthood entails. Their experiences, of course, are as varied as their personalities.

Dexter entered John Jay College in Manhattan but soon dropped out. He has been working with the Children's Defense Fund's youth anti-violence initiative, helping coordinate activities for youngsters in black communities. The Fund staff who recruited Dexter for his job told him they would help him apply to another college. He is eager to leave New York.

Tina has been working at a local restaurant in order to supplement her income from free-lance writing—a difficult way to earn a living even for the most gifted of writers. With a bright start and support from her family, she tries hard, like so many others in this city who come from the lower classes. She needs help from adults, and not just personal or professional advice. "Can I ask an enormous favor?" she asks Terry Williams politely. She needs money to make this month's rent. "I'll pay you back in a month. The restaurant doesn't pay me all that much, you know." She is already providing a rationalization for next month.

"I'm still writing for *Paper* magazine when I can," she tells Terry, "but they don't pay any money. I have a few writing assignments, but some I don't want to do because I would have to change my style. At the restaurant they want me to be day manager, but that won't last because the hours are too long." She tells him about Joyce, who is writing for *The Village Voice*. "We see each other occasionally," Tina says, "and talk on the phone. She's doing really well."

Sheena has found a job, but it is off the books, pays little, and is illegal as far as the welfare department is concerned, since she is still receiving assistance. "I don't want my welfare cut off," Sheena says. "This is one of the first times I've had enough money to buy my daughter a real bed and have plenty of food in the refrigerator too. Right now I'm happier than I've ever been in my life." Nonetheless, she is looking for a new, more secure job.

She confides further that she has met "a nice guy who loves me, and we gonna get married. And I've found God. I go to Bible study once a week and to regular church services on Sundays. The ladies in the church pray for me."

A Last Meeting

At the last meeting of the Writers Crew, all the members felt it was time to talk about the next phase in their lives. They would think about the future, and discuss the journals in which they had recorded their experiences and feelings over the past.

Many of the Crew members thought of these journals as their books, and they had seen fit to give them titles. Dexter came up with *The Life of a Kid on Parole,* while Marisa will probably call her journal *Nicky.* Sheena, who has settled on *Rain Goes Up* as a title for her work, has been impressed by Aaron Sears's accomplishments. "You remember when Aaron read from his piece 'Seer'?" she asks. "Well, he's written like a whole book by now. You should see his stuff."

In his journal, *Before My Time,* Aaron writes about his grandmother and her influence on his life. Sheena tells the Crew that Aaron loved her very much, and considers her a part of his soul. Much of what he is today he can attribute to her. She was a special teacher, and while Aaron understood her teaching, he always tried to tell her that some old lessons needed an extra twist in order for them to be meaningful to a younger generation. She felt that the younger generation didn't listen to the wisdom of the past, and she often thought Aaron did not heed her word. The truth, however, was otherwise: Aaron listened, and applied what he could of her wisdom.

Now that she is dead, Aaron is reminded again and again of her knowledge. Many things she had predicted or commented on indeed have come to pass. Yet there is one thing she would say that Aaron wishes he did not remember. She often repeated that he would be satisfied after she was dead and buried. She would say this usually when, in her opinion, he was being hard-headed; he thought he was just expressing himself. In his journal, Sheena tells the Crew, Aaron has found a new way to express himself. Through it, he hopes, he can pay homage to his grandmother and demonstrate that he is preserving the wisdom she passed on to him.

"We only have one promise to make to each other," Terry Williams tells the Crew. "We should all give something to the next generation."

"Yeah," Sheena agrees, "we should mentor the next group of kids in the Crew."

This first Writers Crew is unanimous. The members hug one another but never really say good-bye. They know it is not the last time they will see one another.

CHAPTER 9

Building
on the Strengths
of the Projects

Dexter, now a member of the Children's Defense Fund's student advisory board and responsible for helping coordinate a nationwide student movement, has never been so excited in his life. He is one of the chosen few, and he knows it. He has just returned from Washington, D.C., where he visited the White House and shook hands with President and Mrs. Clinton. "It was really something," he gushes to Terry Williams. As part of his work with the Fund, Dexter went on a lobbying trip to the nation's capital. Along with other young people from similar backgrounds, some of whom appeared before congressional committees, he was there to advance the cause of national service and to seek emergency funds to address the epidemic of youth violence. A White House reception was to highlight the trip.

The day before he was supposed to leave for Washington, Dexter called Bill Kornblum's office in a panic. He had no clothes to wear to the White House. His graduation suit was too loud for such an august occasion; and he owned no conventional jacket, proper pants, or appropriate tie. Perhaps he should attend only the work sessions and forget about the White House visit. Yet this event was not to be missed. Terry Williams had time to accompany Dexter shopping, and he went to Washington with the proper clothes—even if they were somewhat dull for his taste.

Back in Harlem, Dexter reflects on his experience. "I realize now that the people in Washington were important people. Not that I'm not important now," he says with a big grin. "At first I really thought, 'White House? Big deal. This ain't gonna faze me.' But you know, it did. It was like a dream, meeting all those people, feeling powerful and special. It was really something else. I'm back here in the 'jects, man, and it's a drag, but I know I have work to do." He admits to a great sense of self-worth that people believe in him and rely on his help.

This is a grown-up Dexter talking. He has never expressed himself this way. Despite his maturing, however, he needs support. The question remains whether and how he can continue to grow in an environment he often finds wanting. "I want to give something to my neighborhood," he says, "but I got to get out of here in order to give that something." Dexter struggles with this dilemma. For now he is preparing to go down South as part of his work with the Fund.

Sheena, now living in a housing project in the Bronx, likes her apartment but not the area. Her new job, arranged by her grandmother, isn't as rewarding as she would like, but she's grateful to have a job. "I'm glad I got one 'cause so many other people don't. They don't have anything to do. I help this older woman in her home. I have to clean her, bathe her, clothe her. It's like she's back to a child again. I do this on selected weekdays and some weekends. It pays good, and I have somebody I trust to take care of Xiamara.

"I believe in God and I thank Him for all He's done for me. I go to church more now than I ever did before. I go with my grandmother, and I go with my boyfriend."

Sheena too is moving into an adult role and assuming adult responsibilities. She has put her wild days behind her. She feels like a survivor, and thinks in terms of a career and a secure life for herself and her daughter. Sheena, who would otherwise merely represent a number of categories—minority, teenager, single parent, unemployed, welfare recipient—and corresponding social ills, has charted a path. Welfare was a stepping-stone, a help when she had nowhere else to turn, and she sees the projects as similarly temporary; she hopes to leave them in a few years.

Sheena knows she has been extremely fortunate. She has come through great trials and has found people outside her family who care about her. She has learned to like discussion with others, and that she can be articulate and make people laugh and smile. All of this and the satisfaction she takes from her child give her an inner strength, an emotional armor, to protect her from the dangers and temptations of the street. Sheena may well be following in the footsteps of those strong women in project neighborhoods who organize to safeguard the lives of area youngsters, and thus affect the future.

The Making and Unmaking
of Public Housing Neighborhoods

Rose Cordero often reflects on what makes public housing a decent or difficult place to bring up children. As a well-known tenant organizer in Harlem, she has had the opportunity to visit public housing projects in other areas of New York and in other cities as well. She has seen alternatives in New Orleans, St. Louis, Washington, Cleveland, Chicago, among others, and has been exposed to various ideas and plans for public housing. She mentions congressional bills relating to apartment ownership and tenant management, and the work of Jack Kemp, secretary of housing and urban development under George Bush.

While it may appeal to residents of troubled and mismanaged projects, as Mrs. Cordero knows, the idea of selling off public housing apartments is not popular in New York. Many who know the city's projects believe that sale of the apartments would only diminish the stock of low-income housing in a city already sorely strapped for homes for the poor. Near the Carver project, for example, if they sell at all, nonproject apartments now go for about $10,000 a room. A few blocks downtown, in another neighborhood, they may sell for as much as $350,000 a room. The Housing Act of 1937, which created the federal initiative for public housing, was not passed so that tenants who happened to be on the spot when a purchase offer was made could reap windfall profits from the sale of public property. If there are tenants of Carver, Johnson, King, or any other public housing projects who can afford to buy property, they would be better off investing in the neighborhoods surrounding those the projects. That good investment would also free apartments in public buildings for new tenants. Tenant ownership through a variety of means, including sweat equity, is a welcome idea but not if it diminishes the precious supply of lower-cost housing.

New York City has pioneered in strategies to construct or rehabilitate low-rise buildings with apartments that can be sold to qualified public housing tenants. Were they to be funded on a larger scale, these strategies could create many more vacancies for the thousands of families waiting in squalor to be accepted into existing projects. But lately there has been little hope of adequate funding or even social policy from Washington. The pervasive sense there seems to be that public housing solutions to the crisis of homelessness are doomed to fail.

Indeed, failure has been the rule in many big cities. The chance to see other big-city projects, and their relative success or failure, gave Mrs. Cordero a heightened understanding of New

York's problems, as well as a greater appreciation of its small victories, in public housing. "I wanted to know why people in New York kept saying we had the most successful public housing." After seeing the notorious project neighborhoods of Chicago, St. Louis, and Cleveland, she understood. Abandoned and burned-out apartments and buildings, apartments with bathroom and kitchen fixtures missing—these were typical, and more common than in Harlem. In these cities, she learned, "when people move out, they take things out, plumbing and everything else. And when they take things out, they're not replaced when somebody else moves back in. In New York they're replaced, but not in these other cities. Apartments get boarded up, and people don't want to be the only ones left on their floor."

In Cleveland, Mrs. Cordero felt tenants had "a siege mentality, like 'Let's abandon ship.' I'm going by a building saying, 'Gee, it's really empty here.' And people tell me people live there. And I'm saying people can't be living there 'cause there's no glass in the windows, they're all boarded up. Well, if somebody broke a pane the housing authority wouldn't replace it with glass, they'd replace it with wood. They would say, 'Those people don't know how to take care of glass.' There was wood up all over the place. There were some apartments completely boarded up, because when all the glass was broken out and the stove was broken and the refrigerator wasn't functioning, the person found somewhere else to live. Then somebody would go in and take the rest of the stuff out to fix other people's apartments with. So if that happened along a whole row of houses, soon everything was empty.

"In New York City they can't do that, because there's such a waiting list. There's too many people. These people have no place else to go. But in other cities, where it's not as crowded, there are alternatives."

There are other reasons for differences between many of New York's project neighborhoods and those of other cities. Mrs.

Cordero and other tenant leaders have made participatory politics a key element in New York public housing. The degree of tenant involvement in planning improvements in maintenance and amenities is unheard of in many other large city public housing administrations. New York City Housing Authority architect Len Hopper, a veteran of many years of working with tenants and managers on landscaping and other improvements in the projects, observes that in the well-organized Harlem projects nothing can be done without meetings with the tenants. "You better not order anything to put in those buildings"—even a new color paint—"without first getting together with the tenants. They are interested in everything. Sometimes it can slow things down and everyone may get frustrated, but usually it's for the best. They know how to use their power."

Even in projects where crack dealers terrorize children and adults, where the sound of gunfire shatters the night, tenants—many of them women like Mrs. Cordero—proclaim their opposition to the disruptive elements. Some have been killed for their activism, and when they are, despite the danger, others step forward to fill their places.

Martin Luther King, Jr., Towers in Harlem was notorious during the late 1960s and into the mid-1970s. Efforts by the tenants' organization and the New York City Housing Authority to turn this complex around proved successful in the late 1980s, when King seemed to be safer than many other uptown projects. The children here did better in school than children elsewhere in Harlem, and tenant participation in supporting the project manager was high. King was known in the Housing Authority as a project where efforts to work with local leadership had paid off, where there was a sense of community and political cohesion.

But anyone who spent any time in King could not miss the abandoned tenements across the street from its northern border, boarded-up buildings used as crack houses or locations for dealing. Young people, all out of school and unemployed, maintained a crap game at the curb near the vacant buildings. When King tenants organized a basketball league, with games to be played in a pleasant courtyard well within the project, gambling drug dealers ruined the fun by placing heavy bets on the games. A referee was stabbed during a game when the dealers decided he was biased in favor of the team they were betting against. Not long afterward two King teenagers were killed in a nearby tenement apartment—the murder may have been drug-related—and a child from King was abducted from a playground there and never seen again. These events all took place within a matter of months, and all despite the best efforts of people in the project. These tragedies confirm to project residents their intuitive sense of the limitations of local organizing. The bootstrap remedy to social problems is effective for only so long, and without additional resources from the larger community and nation, even the best tenant organizing may not meet its goals. Faced with the problems of blight and poverty, compounded by sheer density of population, project residents will be unable to make their lives, and those of their children, any easier or more "successful."

Too often in the United States, public housing has served as a means of removing blacks and other minorities. Historical and social scientific evidence shows that blacks and other minorities were often intentionally segregated from the larger society by being placed in public housing projects. While public housing has been a way for the urban poor to escape older decaying tenements and rat-infested alleys, it has just as easily served to forestall integration in housing. The experience of the writer Frank London Brown and his family in 1950s Chicago encapsulates the dual nature of public housing. When one of his children was killed after falling over a rotted banister in their tenement building, Brown was even more anxious to be approved for one of the city's new public housing projects. The Browns were eventually accepted into a low-rise project on the South Side, but they and other black families were met by a hostile white neighborhood. Lines were drawn, and months of rioting and bombing ensued. Increasingly, public housing projects were located in places already racially segregated or likely to become so.

Many of New York's older projects are exceptions to this rule, just as many of those built in the 1960s on the periphery of the city are not. There was racial and ethnic integration in the Harlem projects of the 1950s. It was in those years, in fact, that traditions of local control and tenant militancy were created. Honoring those traditions, speaking in the interests of project residents, arguing for improvements in their quality of life is not the same as defending public housing as a way to maintain segregated urban ghettos. Advocating more concern and more resources to improve existing project neighborhoods is not to suggest that more segregated high-rise housing should be built. Rather, fair housing laws should be enforced, public funding for low-income housing should be increased, and all sensible possibilities that might resolve the plight of project residents should be tried out. The larger society cannot afford to ignore or write off the existing projects, whatever their appearance or prospects, while awaiting more successful social policies.

If we care to make them so, housing projects can be good places for children and adolescents to grow up in. They can become centers for community building and bases for serious efforts to enhance children's safety. The stereotypes of public housing projects as drug-infested war zones and worse may make these seem like unrealistic notions. As the experience of the Writers Crew shows, however, even a small amount of attention and guidance can have a positive impact. Mrs. Johnson, the manager at the King project, talks freely about both the progress and the setbacks she and her tenants have had in trying to build a decent environment for children. Residents are proud of the way the project has "shaped up." They have built community where, originally, "so many poor strangers were just piled on top of each other."

Against Compassion Fatigue

Public housing projects may well be considered high-risk social environments for younger residents: poverty, violence, unwanted pregnancy, drug use and drug dealing, and early death are just some of the dangers. These dangers, Mrs. Johnson points out, are a consequence of the sheer number of poor families concentrated in the projects. Yet they are a consequence also of a history of neglect, and of a pervasive idea that poor youngsters do not deserve the same level of education, training, services, and employment opportunity as youngsters in more affluent neighborhoods.

In Harlem the most immediate "elsewhere" is just below 96th Street. But it would be inaccurate to suggest that these more affluent downtown neighbors do not care or lack commitment. Upper East Side settlement houses and social welfare organizations sponsor numerous programs, directed at the uptown kids. There might be more, but that would require a greater commitment from the larger society. Indifference to the problems of project neighborhoods expands as a function of distance. People in the suburbs are more indifferent or even hostile to the idea of sacrificing on behalf of project residents than are people from the wealthy neighborhoods adjacent to the projects. This is not difficult to understand: the community below 96th Street is more affected by violence and social problems in Harlem than are people in the affluent suburbs; furthermore, suburban dwellers do not share the physical—and at times psychic—space that residents of the same city share, whatever their obvious socioeconomic differences. In many communities outside the inner city "compassion fatigue" or cynicism has set in. Either may be bred by self-serving theories of "benign neglect" or "trickle down," and fueled by a sense of resentment toward "those neighborhoods" and "those kids" who do not deserve special attention.

The social sciences are to blame for rejection of the urban poor as well. The theory of the underclass now popular in academia lends credence to ideas of irredeemability and irreversible damage. But when they attempt to find an underclass in the poor neighborhoods of the city, as opposed to a criminal underworld with its own obverse class ranks, investigators most often bump against the working poor, the unemployed, and the disabled. In the sparse social scientific literature on big-city public housing neighborhoods, life there is equated with welfare dependency, segregation, permanence of the underclass, violence, neglect, and more recently, crack addiction and the marauding of adolescent "wolf packs." For New York City projects at least, this is not an accurate depiction of life in most households. On the rare occasions when sociologists or dedicated journalists make sustained visits to project neighborhoods, in search of "news from the underclass," the broad, objectifying categories of class dissolve in favor of the voices of individuals, real people who are not the convenient personification of a sociological abstraction.

Although the public housing environments identified here are relatively successful, the dangers and risks to adolescents in these areas should not be ignored. All young residents of the projects are in danger these days. And perhaps the greatest danger to them is not the random bullet or the violent gang, but the indifference of a society that does not see the waste of human potential and fails so often to guarantee that doors be opened and remain open for these youngsters.

The population of New York City's housing projects, officially more than 530,000, unofficially well above 630,000, would constitute the nineteenth-largest city in the United States. As centers of dense population whose working residents are in large part in the low-wage sectors of the city's economy, project neighborhoods have been consistently neglected. Project dwellers are thought of as a dependent underclass.

For better or worse, the projects are part of the city; conditions there are significant for the city's future. Yet young people in the projects continue to experience declining education and increasing frustration, alienation, and violence—problems difficult to address, perhaps, and all needless. The risks to adolescents enticed by deviant street life are worse than they have been for many years. Nonetheless, our data do not support the reigning negative stereotypes of life in public housing. Projects in Harlem and elsewhere in New York City are embattled, but they offer opportunities to establish bases of support and address the threat of escalating violence.

The young people of Harlem and communities like it are imperiled to no small degree because of past ghettoizing that accounts for the population density, and thus for the concentration of teenagers and young adults in the projects. There is a limited number of jobs in neighborhood stores and businesses open to them, and elsewhere in the city the picture is just as bleak, if not more so. Entry-level jobs are diminishing, while the competition for what jobs there are increases with the growing presence of foreign workers who are hired at wages lower than the legal minimum. Parents in the projects need help to make their children qualified and competitive in years to come. Whatever other goals it may have, we believe that the benefit of social science should be measured also by whether and how it equips neighborhood residents and their leaders to meet this severe growing crisis.

Public Housing and a Response to the Youth Crisis

Public housing was never intended to be the final, permanent residence for as high a proportion of tenants as it has become in New York and other large cities. The rising tide of economic mobility was supposed to lift families out of public accommodations and into the housing market. Instead there has been an opposite trend: for the past twenty years, often reluctantly, families have brought in relatives or others, even entire families, and doubled up in apartments. Salaries have remained stagnant, buying power has diminished, and rents on the private market have soared.

So what is to be done? First, society's efforts to make the projects the nodes of upward mobility as originally intended should be renewed—if not for adult residents, then at least for the children. This will entail upgrading community centers in the projects so that both adults and children can learn new skills and better avail themselves of the programs that already exist to serve them. It will mean extending networks to link employers with young people and adults in the projects who have been acquiring needed skills. It will require expanding public housing stock through rehabilitation of apartment units in abandoned buildings adjacent to the projects. Such initiatives would necessarily grow out of the largely bootstrap community programs lovingly nurtured by the Montanas and Corderos in the community. Their heroic efforts cry out for more resources. The legislation needed to support and amplify their efforts would qualify under policies now being considered by the Departments of Labor and Housing and Urban Development. Funds targeted for training and comprehensive health programs, which would employ local residents, would be "retail" rather than massive "wholesale" budget items. They would make an enormous difference to the morale and the survival abilities of project families.

Second, as a response to the present youth crisis, experienced youth workers should be assigned to each project. They would work the streets, parks, and schoolyards afternoons and nights, their job to help steer kids away from drugs and violence and into constructive activities in local community centers. Youngsters prone to violence might be introduced to activities to build positively on their physical ability. Those with other problems deemed incorrigible could be identified and selected for more specialized help. Young people who think their lives are irremediably marred by arrest records could be encouraged into education and work programs. Furthermore, the youth workers would try to foster a new sense of pride in Harlem's most troubled and jaded young people. They in turn would pass on the message to friends and siblings—and not just the negative message, against drugs and violence, but also a positive one, about the importance of African-American, Latino, and family heritage in New York and the world.

This proposal, like the first, is not new. And there already have been some attempts at implementing both. Street workers, for example, were deployed during the 1950s and early 1960s with considerable success. And today individuals such as Pedro Pedrazza take it upon themselves to be out where kids gather. Youth workers would not labor blindly or alone; instead they would reach out to link kids with existing community agencies. While their efforts cannot be guaranteed as a solution, they would be invaluable for the lives they might save and the senseless violence they might prevent. It would cost less than $50,000 per worker per year—including training and overhead support—to serve a project, where the average population aged ten to eighteen is at least five hundred, and the adjacent neighborhood, where much of the mob youth is recruited.

Of course, more than just one measure must be taken to meet the youth crisis. Above all, there is the need never to stop giving young people a hand and a chance to work toward a better life. There are short-term measures—for instance a grassroots effort to get kids to turn in their guns to the police—as well as long-term approaches—such as those that involve facilitating mobility in the projects and surrounding neighborhoods. Often younger residents need a chance to leave the community, to visit relatives in rural areas, or to work or attend an educational program outside the city. Through commitments to national service, community redevelopment grants, special education incentives and loan programs, and a wide array of comprehensive health initiatives, these opportunities can be opened, and the effects of years of cynicism and neglect can be reversed.

Will such initiatives cause further resentment in middle-class communities? Perhaps they will, in some cases, but if the initiatives are developed so that all communities with poor neighborhoods can qualify for help, all such communities—be they small town or big city—will stand to benefit. We believe that immediate initiatives on behalf of federal housing project neighborhoods, if successful, can serve as models for other communities. The sheer density of youth population in the projects warrants this immediate concern.

Almost miraculously, as he thinks about it now, Dexter is following in the path of more conventionally gifted project kids such as Marcus and Joyce. Like them he is on a route which promises a better life beyond the Harlem streets. And also like them, he faces the agonizing confrontation with his "twoness." The divided self of the African-American child, as W. E. B. Du Bois originally pointed out, is incubated in the segregated ghetto on the one hand, and the need, too often not met, of the growing child to master the language and culture of the white world, on the other. If Dexter and all the other members of the Writers Crew had their way, they would be given far more of a chance to resolve the duality of life in America within their own communities. The uptown kids have a great deal to offer America. They yearn for the chance to serve both black and white worlds without being forced to sever their attachments to home and loved ones.

Epilogue

SHEENA lives in a Bronx public housing project and works full-time as a home care attendant.

MARCUS completed his master's degree at the University of Michigan and is pursuing his doctorate in political science. He works at the Michigan Office of Equal Opportunity.

MARISA lives with her husband in the Bronx. She now has two children.

BUDD lives in Greenwich Village.

TINA attends Bryn Mawr. She continues to write for *Paper* magazine.

JOYCE teaches a course on writing at the New School for Social Research in New York and writes for *Vibe* magazine.

AARON lives in King Towers and is completing his epic about the projects.

PACO works as graphic artist for an art-publishing company.

DEXTER plans to attend Shaw College in North Carolina.

JACK is in jail in Texas.

Index